Learning to Love

In 27 Days

By Dr. Norman R. Wise

Dear Angie

May the love of God fill
you and that love learn
you quickly fight I appreciate
you being a partner for us

Ah - Dr. ?

Learning to Love in 27 days

Introduction: Learning to Love in 27 days

The most difficult task we have in our lives is to love. Love is the difference between success and failure. If we live a life of love, we are a success. If we do not live a life of love, we are a failure.

The reality is we don't live in such a black and white world. We live in a life of grey. Sometimes, we love and are successful. Sometimes, we do not love and fail. Never is our love perfect. We know only substantial and partial success at loving. Yet, it is our duty and desire to love and love well. One of the most felt needs of our lives is to love and be loved.

I have been teaching on the book of Romans for several years now. As I was teaching this book, I came across a section that was focused on love in Romans 12:9-21 which begins with a challenge to love without hypocrisy. Like the better known passage in 1 Corinthians 13, we have in this section a practical outline of what a life of love would look like for a Christian. This life of love includes loving God and loving others. As I read it I found 27 challenges to love.

The question for me was how to best bring these 27 challenges to my congregation. I considered a series of 27 sermons, but that did not seem to me to be a realistic approach to having them practically apply this great section of scripture to their lives. As I prayed about what to do, it came to me that I could challenge them to read one challenge a day for a month. In addition, I could write 27 e-mail devotionals that could be read each day to reinforce the message of this passage of scripture. Then at our joint worship service at the end of the month, we would have a share time of how God had moved people to love more effectively through meditation on these biblical challenges to love. Those who participated in that process did, in fact, grow in 27 days to love more effectively.

It struck me later that others might gain from the same process that our church went through. So in the desire to see more people learn to love more effectively, I have written this book with a prayer that it will lead us all to love more. I hope this is a blessing to you.

Each chapter will have a meditation on one challenge. The best way to read this book is slowly. Read just one day at a time. Take time to put your thoughts and feelings down in the journaling section provided after each chapter. Write up a "love goal" for the day and try to take a small but real step in learning to love.

Use this book for your daily devotions for one month and I believe that God will bless you with a greater ability to love HIM and to love others. In the end, all that matters is that we love, so learning how to love is the most important skill we could ever attain. May, this book help you in your quest to love.

Learning to Love: Day One: Romans 12:9

Let love be genuine ... ESV

Let love be without hypocrisy ... ASV

Be sincere in your love for others ... CEV

Love is not a hypocrite.

The Greek word here translated genuine, without hypocrisy, or sincere is *anupokritos* which is defined as meaning to be without pretense, genuine, sincere, or literally to be 'without play-acting. It means that love must come out of true commitment and affection. We should not just be playing a role in the drama of life. We are not to see ourselves as actors on a stage or in a movie but real people in the real world who strive to really love.

This verse stresses the need of love to be authentic and not faked. This idea of real and sincere love is most likely best reflected in the Old Testament by the idea of "steadfast love" (Gen 24:12) and is seen about 396 times in the Old Testament. This Hebrew word for this idea is *chesed*. It means a grace filled love that is loyal and refuses to give up.

False love is without grace, without persistence, and without loyalty. God loves His people based on grace, persistently, and with full loyalty. False love is conditional, short lived, and without commitment.

What keeps my love from being sincere and genuine? Sometimes, it is because I am just so tired and worn out that I have lost touch with any love in my soul. Because I do not keep my Sabbath rest and focus on the love of God for me, my inner self becomes empty and barren. Outwardly, I can "play act" my roles in a loving way but inwardly there simply is nothing to fuel true love or compassion. I can see that to be genuine and sincere in love. I would have to slow down and spend more time in gospel-centered, private and public worship. My love must be fueled by God's love if it is to be real, substantial, and lasting.

What keeps my love from being sincere and genuine? Sometimes it is because I have legalistically made it conditional. Instead of having it soaked in God's grace, I have it soaked in my own rules of righteousness. I judge and condemn others. It is easy to judge and condemn other people. This is because we are all sinners. Everyone can justly be condemned and damned. As I stand in righteous indignation and allow my human anger to grow within me at the failures of others then love dries up. My love becomes not a gift I give but a reward I offer to those who can perform. Unfortunately, my conditional love encourages people to "play act" with me. So then I both fail to love and am rarely sincerely loved; once I have twisted "love" to be a conditional acceptance based upon my subjective standards. Soon I am left with "all of life is a stage and we are but players upon it" and authenticity in relationships has died. Legalism kills true relationships.

I have been loved unconditionally at times. There have been people who have consistently had compassion on me both on my good and bad days. A small handful of people have given me this precious gift of sincere and genuine grace based love.

The greatest example of this type of love for me was shown when God poured out His love on me without condition in sending Jesus the Messiah to die for my sins. That is the greatest act of sincere love ever demonstrated before a cynical world.

The reality of this love was demonstrated to me at the times when I was at my lowest point and people reached out to help me. These people who lifted me up when I was most in despair were a vital link to me seeing God's love for me. They became physical representations of God's love to me.

It is good to remember those moments when people demonstrated sincere, grace filled love towards me. These are the richest moments of my life, even when they were also the times when I was the most bankrupt emotionally and spiritually. Such memories remind me of just how amazing love can be.

All this talk about love being real reminded me of the "Velveteen Rabbit" a story I read to my children when they were young. That story talks about the need of real love. In the book there is a conversation between the toy rabbit and the rocking horse:

"What is REAL?" asked the Rabbit one day, when they were lying side by side near the nursery fender, before Nana came to tidy the room. "Does it mean having things that buzz inside you and a stick-out handle?"

"Real isn't how you are made," said the Skin Horse. "It's a thing that happens to you. When a child loves you for a long, long time, not just to play with, but REALLY loves you, then you become Real."

"Does it hurt?" asked the Rabbit.

"Sometimes," said the Skin Horse, for he was always truthful. "When you are Real you don't mind being hurt."

"Does it happen all at once, like being wound up," he asked, "or bit by bit?"

"It doesn't happen all at once," said the Skin Horse. "You become. It takes a long time. That's why it doesn't happen often to people who break easily, or have sharp edges, or who have to be carefully kept. Generally, by the time you are Real, most of your hair has been loved off, and your eyes drop out and you get loose in the joints and very shabby. But these things don't matter at all, because once you are Real you can't be ugly, except to people who don't understand." [1]

I think that for us to become real we have to be aware of the love of God for a very long time. We have to walk with God in the love of the gospel. As we do this in the midst of a very difficult life, we begin to know what it is to really love even as we have been really loved by our Messiah Jesus and our Heavenly Father. As we go through that process, then we begin to avoid faking love while more and more find ourselves feeling real love.

Make a list of ways that you "fake love". How could you make love more real in these relationships? Write up a plan to become more sincere in your expressions of love.

---

[1] http://digital.library.upenn.edu/women/williams/rabbit/rabbit.html

A prayer: Lord, fill my heart with your steadfast love. Holy Spirit, sing in my soul the song of your love found in Messiah Jesus. Open my eyes that I might see the wonder of your great and graceful love for me. Help me to refuel and have the energy to love. Keep me from being a "play actor" but help me to really live life and really love you and others made in your image.   Let me be real.

My Love Goal for the Day is: _____

Journaling Notes for Day One

Learning to Love: Day Two – Romans 12:9

Abhor what is evil (ESV)

Hate everything that is evil (CEV)

Loath every attitude and action that brings death and pain into the world (Norm Wise paraphrase)

True love knows how to hate.

The Greek word for abhor or hate is apostugeo. The word stugeo is one that means to openly express anger. The preposition άπό *away from*, may either denote *separation* or be merely *intensive*. An intense sentiment is meant: *loathing*. Our emotional reaction to evil is to be an open expression of disgust and avoidance. This word is strong and intense. It means a passionate sentiment of hatred and repulsion against its object.

The word for evil here is poneros. It seems to be a word that focuses on actions and attitudes that cause pain and trouble. *Poneros* in Modern Greek means one whose mind tends toward evil, a sly underhanded person, or even one with a "dirty" mind. The word is related to the word *ponos*, which means pain. Both pain and *poneros* (as well as the English derivatives "penitence" and "penitentiary") come from the ancient root "*penomai*" meaning "to exert effort" for the purpose of being hurtful and damaging.

Pain is the result of this "effort", and the poneric person (or *poneros*) is its propagator. Actually, "effort" is not precisely the right word. *Penomai* is something I do to myself that wears me down, that harms me and makes me suffer. In other words, it is an imposition of death upon my person by my person. We can, therefore, understand the poneric person as a propagator of self-generated death. The person who is a *poneros* is not simply someone who acts to cause pain, but a state of being filled with moral death that perpetuates itself. Biblically, this was identified as the "devil" as "the evil one".

The word speaks deeply of the fall of humanity and the curse of God upon our unfaithful labors. It speaks of the connection between moral rebellion and death. Doing what is not God's will can only produce pain to others and me. There is no hope that evil will actually bless anyone. It should be avoided like the plague.

Imagine if you were on the operating table and were being given blood. What if the doctor told you that they had purposely chosen blood that had the HIV virus in it to give to you? The purpose was to infect you with HIV. How strongly would you abhor and hate the blood coming into your body? How much would you fight to get free? That is how we should react to moral evil.

Ps 97:10 - Hate evil, you who love the LORD,

Pr 8:13 - The fear of the LORD is to hate evil; ...

Amos 5:15 - Hate evil, love good, And establish justice in the gate!

We live in a time that is apathetic towards moral evil. We have denied that real and objective moral evil exists. We simply believe there are different strokes for different folks. We pride ourselves on being tolerant and wise in understanding that there are not absolute moral standards. We have become free of any idea of absolute good and evil.

We have seared our conscience and it responds less and less strongly to moral depravity. Rarely do we "abhor" anything. Relative truth has led to relative morals and this has led to moral apathy. It is hard to get our energy up to strongly oppose evil either in our souls or our society. We would never connect being a loving person with having a strong hatred of evil.

Now some evil I do abhor. That is the evil I find distasteful. Most of the time it is not what tempts me but it is what I abhor in others. It allows me to see myself as self righteous and morally superior. This is because in this particular case I do not like the taste of that particular sin. I would hate it even if God did not exist.

However, the real danger to my soul is the evil that I do not abhor. It is the evil that tempts me. It is those things that God has said that are evil that I feel are good. I justify the pain they cause by focusing on the joy they bring to me.

Then there are those things I hate. But I keep doing them even though I know they cause pain to those I love and to me. I feel addicted and trapped. I am infected with these sins and they will not leave me regardless of all my efforts.

"For I do not understand my own actions. For I do not do what I want, but I do the very thing I hate." (Romans 7:15 ESV)

Only by seeing sin as the source of pain and death can I abhor it as I should abhor it. Only by not becoming lost in the false advertising about the benefits of evil can I see it for what it is, poison. The world, the flesh, and the devil all strive to keep me from this reality. They desire me to buy into the lies about moral depravity and not fight against moral evil with all my being. I must declare war on sin in my soul if I am to become a person controlled by love.

Evil is what put Messiah Jesus on the cross. Evil is what caused his suffering. Evil caused the pain of Messiah Jesus. I should hate evil just because of what it did to my Lord Jesus.

Make a list of the evil you have a peace treaty with. These would be sins that you justify or have stopped fighting. These are temptations that easily take you. Once you have made this list then ask God to give you hatred for these sins.

Prayer

Lord, help me to see moral evil for what it is in reality. Let me see evil as a cancer that must be radically removed from my being. I must respond to it without compromise. It must die or it will kill me. Lord, increase my hatred of sin, transgression, wrong, lust, greed, selfishness, lies, and evil. Give me energy to fight sin within my soul and in society. Lord, have mercy and fill me with holy hatred. Give me your love for righteousness. Amen

My Love Goal for the Day is:

Journal Day Two

Learning to love – Day Three

... hold fast what is good. (ESV)

... cleave to that which is good (ASV)

... hold tight to everything that is good (CEV)

Cling to that which is good. (EMTV)

Love clings to goodness.

Now we are not saved by our good works. We are saved from hell by the grace of God alone through Christ Jesus' death, burial, and resurrection that have paid for our sins. Salvation is a free gift.   This is one of the main teachings of Paul in the book of Romans.

However the reason we are saved by grace, is due to the lack of good works in our life and not because God does not take pleasure in our doing good deeds. We have been saved by God's grace alone by the death of Messiah Jesus for us. Now that we have been saved, God has ordained us to live a life full of good works (Eph 2:8-10). We do good deeds not be saved but because we are saved.

The Greek word here for "hold fast" is *killao* which is literally "glue". The idea expressed here is that we should strive to forever attach ourselves to the good. We are to glue ourselves to the good or *agathos*. We are to become fully attached to virtue, health, usefulness, excellence, honor and that which brings true joyfulness into the world.

We are to run from in horror the moral depravity that causes pain and death. We are to run passionately after moral good which causes true joy and brings life.   We are to desire to become so attached to good that it would be like being "super glued" to something.   We are to be unable to get rid of it without a lot of pain and trouble.   To do what is morally good is to be and act like Messiah Jesus. It is to love God first and then have compassion on people. It is to live a sane, stable, and spiritual life consistently.

How can we get "glued to good"?   Here are some ideas:

1. Wear goodness - This would mean first of all to dress in a modest way. It would mean for married people to keep their wedding bands on.   It would mean to have something that reminds you of your relationship with Christ with you at all times. It could mean wearing a cross around your neck or have a motivational idea on a 3x5 card in my wallet. What can I do that will "glue goodness" to my appearance, dress, and routine of getting ready for daily life? That is the important question for me to answer.

2. Read and talk about goodness to yourself. Watch what you are saying to yourself and make sure what you are saying is moving you in the direction of virtue and not vice.   Talk to yourself about the goodness of God in dying for your sins in the person of Messiah Jesus.   Remind yourself of the good character of God. Read the Bible and other devotional books which call upon you to seek goodness and run from evil.

3. Have your entertainment encourage being "glued to goodness" and not a temptation to vice.   Entertainment has a lot to do with what we become "glued to" in our emotions and actions.   Seek to find fun ways to seek a sane, stable, and healthy life.   Some entertainment encourages our dark side while some fun activities help us appreciate living well. Is the music in your life encouraging virtue or vice?

4. Seek out relationships with people who encourage you being good. Bad company ruins good morals.   We need people who will be "rubbing us the right way" and being cheer leaders for right behavior. This is one of the aspects of attending a small group since people can hold us accountable to what we know to be "good."

5. Make every meal a time to ask God to help you be filled with the Holy Spirit and seek first the Kingdom of God.   By turning every meal into a reminder of God's love for us and our need to love Him, this allows us to become "glued to goodness".

6. Make up self talk that summarizes all the benefits of doing good. Read this self talk as part of your meal time and morning devotions. Sell yourself on the wisdom of doing what is morally noble over compromising with your darker desires. Fall in love with goodness.

7. Talk about good things with other people. Strive to take the "high moral ground" in conversations. Confess desire to do evil as wrong. Do not play with bad attitudes by expressing approval of wrong doing. Be a person who will counsel good behavior and wise living even when you struggle to do it.

8. Be alert to the opportunity to do good. Goodness will remain very abstract until we just "do it". By visiting the lonely, feeding the sick, encouraging the discouraged, giving to the poor, worshipping God with passion, sharing the gospel with the lost, giving wise counsel to the confused, and praying for those in need, we become "glued to goodness" because it becomes a lifestyle.

9.   Bathe yourself in reminders to be and do good. Have signs, posters, art, and rituals which remind you that because of Christ's goodness to you that now you desire to be good. Put reminders to do good and be good into your daily calendar.

10.   Become sensitive to the "clues" that you are beginning to backslide. Keep a radical moral inventory of your life up to date. Most of us become "unglued" over a long period of time. Our attachments to God's will for our life is something lost by erosion rather than a radical decision to do evil.   We simply stop reinforcing our commitment to goodness and then one day we notice we are in a very bad place morally and spiritually.

Finally, beware of one more danger. Ignore anyone who says you are being too "religious" or taking seeking goodness to extremes.   None of us on judgment day will be sad because we gained some virtue but many of us will regret the vices that still dominated our lives.

Prayer

Lord, help me become glued to goodness this day.   Let me build emotional attachments to what is sane, stable, and spiritual. Let me fall madly in love with the good.   Amen

Self Talk Promoting Goodness – Read this six time a day for 27 days

Being good saves me from the pain of guilt.

Being good expresses my love for God and Christ.

Being good shows I am grateful for my sins being forgiven.

I want people to talk about the good I did at my funeral; not make excuses for my vices.

I don't want my children and grandchildren using me as an excuse for destroying their lives.

What would I want to say to the Lord I did in this life when I see HIM face to face? Commit yourself to doing that today!

Being good is emotionally healthy.

Being good is mentally healthy.

Being good is spiritually healthy.

Being good is physically healthy.

Being good produces inner peace.

Being good produces positive self esteem.

Being good produces a positive reputation.

Being good is its own reward.

My Love Goal for the Day is:

Journal Day Three

Day Four: Romans 12:10

Love one another with brotherly affection ... ESV

In love of the brethern be tenderly affectioned one to another ... ASV

Love each other as brothers and sisters ... CEV

Loving one another with the charity of brotherhood ... DRB

Be warmly affectionate to one another with brotherly love ... EMTV

Love one another warmly as Christians .... GNB

Be devoted to each other with mutual affection ... ISV

Love is loyal and intimate.

In English, we might not see much difference between Romans 12:9 where we are told to love without hypocrisy and Romans 12:10 where we are told to love one another.

But in the Greek you have different words used. Romans 12:9 is talking about "agape" love which is affection not based on performance and which indicates a calculated love based on making something the highest priority of our lives. It can be, and most of the time is, highly emotional; but, it is emotion based on personal commitment. Agape love is not superior to other type of love. It simply is a different type or aspect of love.

In this light, one could understand Romans 12:9 as "Don't pretend to have the love of God and others as your highest priority when it really isn't."

Now in Romans 12:10, we have two other Greek words used for love. One is *philostorgos* which is an old compound word used only here in the New Testament and *philadelphia*. Paul is now focusing on the idea that we are to not only reflect God's agape love but also to give to fellow Christians both *philos* and *storgos* love as well.

What is *storgos*? It is a love and loyalty based on a relationship outside of our control. It is the unconditional and long lasting love of family members for one another regardless of personality differences or performance.   It is an affection that is given because of a unity we have with people that was simply destined by the providence of God alone.

In this context, Paul is saying we should feel affection for other Christians because God has chosen them to be our spiritual family. We are to give them loyalty, care, and warmth as we would family members because God has made them part of the visible church. The church is our spiritual family and we owe every member of it the loyal, unconditional love of family.

Philadelphia is a word that strengthens this. *Philos* is when we actively pursue having deep and intimate family relationships. *Storgos* is the foundation for such a pursuit. But *philos* is opening our hearts to feel deep love towards our family members and seeking intimate friendship with them. Here is a commitment to emotional intimacy.

Now context always rules the shades of meaning these words may have. Here we have a call by Paul for Christians to recognize that the gospel of grace has made us a spiritual family with a responsibility to love each other. This relationship means we must open ourselves up to this new set of relationships found in the church and embrace other believers as relatives. This spiritual family is to have as much loyalty given to it as we would give to our physical families. It also means that we must be seeking to make those in our local church, the ones with whom we would have emotionally intimate friendships. Ultimately, these verses can only be experienced in the local church. We are to be ready to embrace any Christian at any time as a family member and have a general attitude towards them which would be one of compassion and empathy. But it is in the company of believers with which we worship that these words will take on concrete and real meaning.

The gospel calls us to make our local church the center of our social life. We are to be a company of friends who have faith in Messiah Jesus as our common bond. Our love for HIM is to create love for one another.

At the present moment, 39% of Americans attend church once a week. It would seem that weekly attendance at church would be the minimum effort people would have to make the local church the center of their social lives. We know that many who attend weekly have not done that.

If we use the normal 80/20 rule, we could speculate that in reality only about 8% of Christians in America have most likely made the relationships at church the central and most important relationships in their lives. Only 8% are experiencing to some degree the reality of what the Apostle Paul wants us to experience in our local church. We must recognize that the church can never be the community of committed love when only 8% of the body of Christ is striving to engage each other in dynamic and real relationships.

How can we open ourselves up to such intimate spiritual friendships? This is hard for many of us because at times we have been hurt in church and been disappointed by "hypocritical love". For many of us from dysfunctional families we have found the church to just be an extension of the dysfunctional and painful relationships we experienced in our homes. Some of us came to the church hoping to find a safe "family" only to be emotionally wounded again but this time in the name of "God". Yet, this pain does not justify us avoiding spiritual friendships.

So we must seek effective ways to relate to each other in the body of Christ. Small groups within the church create a good framework out of which we might be able to develop these types of relationships. It is vital that we seek to know how to experience an emotionally healthy spirituality and have an emotionally healthy church life.

It is God's will that we give ourselves to this spiritual family and yet it is hard to do and harder yet to experience. All that we can strive to do is to be an emotionally healthy Christian and to treat others with respect and love. If each of us strives to practice mature and balanced relationships with other Christians then there is a hope we could begin to see the love of God manifested in a practical way in the local church.

To learn to love, we must be willing to commit to seeking significant and real spiritual friendships in the church. This means we must attend church regularly. It means we need to be part of a small group who shares their lives, struggles, and faith together. Time will have to be given to doing things with others in our fellowship and being transparent to a group of believers. We must seek to serve others and allow others to serve us in times of weakness. Relationships are a two way street and require us to serve others and able to be humble enough to ask for help. Out of this dynamic interaction God in his grace may allow us to actually experience a spiritual bond with others. We must seek to experience loyal and intimate love with each other.

Prayer

Lord, help me get over my fear of being hurt again. Guide me to be an emotionally healthy person who can effectively give love to others and receive love from others. Help me to see that You have created a bond with other Christians and that I am called to experience that spiritual bond and make it real in my daily experience. Lord, help me to give my heart to other Christians.

My Love Goal for the Day is:

Journal for day four:

Day Five: Romans 12:10

Outdo one another in showing honor (ESV)

... in honor preferring one another (ASV)

... honor others more than you do yourself (CEV)

... be eager to show respect for one another. (GNB)

Excel in showing respect for each other (ISV)

Love gives honor to others and never degrades another person.

The verb here is *proegeomai* and means to go before and show the way. It means to be a leader by being the first one who moves forward. It is used only here in the New Testament.

The picture is to strive to outdo each other in speaking well of one another. It is in sincerely complimenting each other, speaking kind words to each other, not gossiping about each other, not verbally abusing each other, and confronting each other in a loving and respectful ways when there are conflicts.   We are to treat each other well in the family of God. The church is to be a place of emotional intimacy that is safe from emotional abuse.

To honor someone is to treat them as valuable. It is to see them as significant and worthy of being treated without abuse.   We are to honor all human beings because they have been made in the image of God. To curse a human being is to curse God (James 3:9). We are to honor every Christian because Messiah Jesus died for them and they have been chosen by God to believe in the Messiah. They are to be treated as God's beloved elect.   God has honored them by choosing them to be saved and having His Son die for them. Therefore, they are to be treated with great honor and respect.

Here again we have the word *allēlōn* which means "one another" and which speaks of the special care and relationships we are to have for each other in the community of believers.   There are many relational responsibilities we have towards "one another" as Christians.   God does not desire there to be any "lone ranger" Christians.

In what ways do we fail to honor other Christians?   Are there people in our local church for whom we fail to express respect?   Are we verbally abusive towards some people in our fellowship?   Do we dishonor some people behind their backs?   Would we be embarrassed if they would appear suddenly in the room when we are speaking about them to others? Do we gossip? How many times do we compliment the people in our fellowship? Do we seek to deal with conflict in a healthy and respectful manner? Are we abusive in any way in our relationships with other believers? These are the questions we need to ask ourselves.

It is hard to have an emotionally healthy fellowship in the church. It is a rare thing to experience in our lives. Yet, that type of loving fellowship is the greatest evidence of the truth of the Christian gospel that exists on this planet.

We live in a culture that sees virtue in being "rude". Letting it "all hang out" and avoiding being "fake" is good from the viewpoint of avoiding hypocritical love but is destructive in that it does not deal with the danger of us expressing our feelings in abusive ways. It also encourages a type of self righteousness in which we pass judgments on others and condemn them in the strongest language without regret. Our culture has very little understanding of honor, respect, or treating people as intrinsically valuable.

Our culture would say that honor and respect have to be earned and are not just given. You may make yourself valuable by your deeds but you have no value by just being conceived. The idea that God sees each person as valuable has little emotional or cultural weight for most people. Few people treat people well because they believe they are made in God's image.

Therefore, it is hard for us to obey this passage. Our culture encourages abusive relationships and this way of dealing with people does not stop when we become Christians. Many of us are not aware when we are being emotionally abusive to others. We do treat Christians the way we would treat family members. The problem is we have been abusive to our families and now are abusive to those in the church in the same way we are at home. If the family life of Christians is not free of emotional and verbal abuse, there is little hope that they will be able to treat people in the church with honor or respect.

We must seek the Lord to help us to become emotionally healthy Christians so that we can express His love to one another in the local church. Make a list of those you have gossiped about in the last month. Ask God for the strength to not gossip about them anymore. Make a list of good attributes for each person about whom you have gossiped. Look for an opportunity to privately or publically praise this person for this virtue that God has given them. Build them up and look at the glass half full when you think of them. If there are issues that must be handled then ask for wisdom to talk to them privately about it. Seek to speak the truth in love. To love we must show respect.

Prayer

Lord, help me to honor every Christian brother or sister in my life. Keep me from gossip. Save me from a self righteous and negative attitude. Let me see that love speaks words of honor and does not seek to condemn those who are accepted and forgiven by God. Amen.

My Love Goal for the Day is:

Journal for Day Five

Day Six – Romans 12:11

Not slothful in business (ESV)

... in diligence not slothful (ASV)

Never give up (CEV)

In carefulness not slothful (DRB)

... not lagging in diligence (EMTV)

Work hard and do not be lazy (GNB)

Never be lazy in showing such devotion. (ISV)

Love is persistent and hard working.

Here we understand that love works hard. Godly passion makes us focused, hardworking, and purpose driven. The gospel says we are not saved by works but calls us to work.

Oknerous the word translated lazy or slothful describes those who are slow due to hesitation, anxiety, or negligence. It is used in the Old Testament in Proverbs 6:6&9 of those who allow inconveniences to stop them or never move from the idea of a good action to actually do something about it (Proverbs 20:4; 21:25). Jesus the Messiah warns us of such an attitude when he says:

"But his master answered him, 'You wicked and SLOTHFUL SERVANT! *You knew that I reap where I have not sown and gather where I scattered no seed? (Matthew 25:26 ESV)*

It is not wise to claim to be a disciple if we hesitate to put our gifts to work and fail to live up to our eternal responsibilities.

The word translated "business" or "diligence" is the Greek word *spoude* which literally means speed or haste. Literally this verse would be "to not be slow in being speedy". But the word implies speaking or acting seriously. Doing what ought to be done as faithfully as we can do it. The meaning seems to be that we are not to be slow in doing what God wants to be the top priorities of our life.

The gospel calls us to a serious life. God has had to send His SON to die for our sins. God is serious about saving us. He wants us to share HIS seriousness by being sober and clear-headed people who are living disciplined and focused lives. We are to be focused on passionately seeking first God's kingdom and righteousness.

It is not easy to remain serious. We live in a culture that values entertainment and much of that entertainment makes us apathetic about seeking righteousness. Happiness is for us the opposite of being serious. Happiness is for many of us the opposite of being righteous. Yet, only in being serious in our pursuit of holiness can we know joy.

For some of us, we have been striving for decades to follow Christ. It is hard to keep the energy up. We sometimes lose heart. We feel the pressure reflected in the book of Ecclesiastes. We hear the song of "Vanity, Vanity, all is Vanity" ringing in our ears and we begin slowing down in our seeking to be filled with God's love and righteousness. Our acts of faith become tempered by fear of failure and cynicism has us abandon doing what we know God has called us to do. Yet, regardless of how long and difficult the race is, we must never give up.

By remembering what God has done for us and has given us in Messiah Jesus we can keep ourselves focused on God's purpose and plan for our lives. The Lord who has started a good work in us will finish it. If we pursue God's love, we cannot fail.

In 1941, Prime Minister Winston Churchill spoke to a school. The days were dark. The power of Nazism seemed impossible to stop. It would be easy to give up. It would be easy to surrender. In the midst of those dark and desperate times, the Prime Minister spoke these words:

"Never give in. Never give in. Never, never, never, never--in nothing, great or small, large or petty--never give in, except to convictions of honor and good sense. Never yield to force. Never yield to the apparently overwhelming might of the enemy."

We are in a battle against the world, the flesh, and the devil. The enemy is telling us to give up. The evil choir sings to us songs urging us to give in and choose the broad and easy way. How can we hope to make a difference in the middle of such a dark and broken world?

Yet, we must remember Nazism did not win. God's kingdom will come and God's purpose will be done on this planet. We must never yield to evil and we must remain faithful in doing our duty with diligence, focus, and faith. God's love will ultimately win.

List the things that take the wind out of your sails and discourage you in your pursuit of holiness. Ask God to overcome each item on that list. See that as a list of your greatest enemies and begin to seek new ways to overcome each one of them.

This reminds me of a hymn I sang as a child:

"This is my Father's world. O let me ne'er forget that though the wrong seems oft so strong, God is the ruler yet." - Maltbie D. Babcock – "This Is My Father's World" 1901.

We will need to review our performance. Then we need to sing to ourselves the song of God's victory in Christ. As our morale rallies, we will find that we can find new strength to press on and "never give in, never give in, never, never, never, never ..."

Love never fails.

Prayer

Dear Lord, You know that I am weary and worn out. You know that the last few defeats have discouraged my heart. I do not know if I can keep going. But Lord, give me the strength to never give up. Give me a holy stubbornness against evil. Put the wind at my back and help me in my weakest hour. Let me see that the only defeat would be in quitting. Lord, don't let me quit! Amen.

My Love Goal for the Day is:

Journal for Day Six

Day Seven – Romans 12:11

Be fervent in spirit (ESV)

Eagerly follow the Holy Spirit (CSV)

In spirit fervent (DRB)

Be on fire with the Spirit (ISV)

Love is on fire.

The word for "fervent" is the Greek word *"zeo"* which means to be hot. For liquids, it means that they are boiling. For solids like metals, it means they are glowing. Perhaps the best way to say this is that this word means to "be fired up". Now the word spirit here can speak of either the "Holy Spirit" or the human spirit. It would appear that the main idea would to "be passionate".

This would mean that we should put our hearts into being wildly faithful. Not only should we not be slow to do our duty, we need to really be excited about doing what God wants in our life. Now such passion we would see as the fruit of the Holy Spirit in our lives, but it also tells us that we must be ready to put emotional energy into our Christian living.

It is amazing how so much stoic philosophy has entered into the church. The idea of Christian spirituality being a desire to remove ourselves from our emotions and being freed of passions is simply not a biblical idea. The problem is not passion but what we are passionate about?

But how do we find passion? Passion comes from purpose and from relationships. You must define concretely what you believe the Lord has called you do to. Ultimately, our purpose must be to follow Messiah Jesus. His purpose must be our purpose. Our passion will only come as we look at HIS passion for us in suffering for our sins. There must be some process by which we begin to define our daily living in light of His kingdom, His righteousness, and our relationship with Him.

There is a story that comes to mind when I think about passion.

There was a prince who was riding down a road. He found a man making bricks. The work was hard, dirty, and hot. The Prince rode up to the man and asked him what he was doing. The man looked up with sweat in his eyes, dirty, and tired. He worked without smiling and his movements were almost mechanical. With a cynical tone the man replied "I am making bricks as any fool can see." and he went back to his work with a look of disgust on his face.

The Prince rode down the road a little bit further and found another man making brick. He also was sweaty and dirty. However, his movements seemed more like he was dancing than working. The Prince rode up and asked the man what he was doing? The man looked up with sweat in his eyes and a smile on his face. He looked in the distance and said "I am building a cathedral!" The man then laughed with joy and went back to making his bricks.

The Prince rode off and marveled at how two men who did the same thing could view their daily labor so differently.

When we connect our duty to the gospel, we glow with God's passion. Our labor becomes a reflection of God's love. The story we tell ourselves about our lives will either drain us of passion or fuel a fire within that has to boil over into action. When God's story of the gospel becomes personally intertwined with our story, this sparks fire within us and we have passion to do God's will.

This is why worship is so vital to finding passion. In experiencing God in worship and hearing the story of His love, we can rekindle the flames of faith and find the passion to love. Go to worship this week seeking to catch God's fire in your heart.

Prayer

Dear Father, I need Your fire in my heart. My passion has become drained. I need You to renew my vision of Your wild love for me. You love me more than I have every imagined. Let my vision of Your love grow as I worship You. Amen

My Love Goal for the Day is:

Journal for Day Seven

Learning to Love - Day Eight – Romans 12:11

Serve the Lord (ESV)

Love serves.

Literally, this verse says for us to be in voluntary slavery and bondage to the Lord. It is a call to act and live with Messiah Jesus as the supreme authority of our lives. We are to surrender all to Messiah Jesus. Every action, word, and attitude is to be controlled by the Messiah Jesus. We are to see everything we do from the moment we rise in the morning till when we sleep at night to be one of service as devoted voluntary slaves. The focus of love is "not my will but your will be done."

This entire concept is hard for us. The idea of a person being in voluntary slavery is very foreign to us. Slavery is evil and bad. Under all normal situations we oppose slavery. Yet now at the very heart of our faith is a command to be a slave. To volunteer to be a slave to Messiah Jesus is a critical part of our life of love. The more we understand His love for us the more we will want to be enslaved to Him.

There are many things that have to be said here. The slavery being offered here is one of being a servant in a family that one has chosen to love. This was called a "bond servant" in the Old Testament. It was a slave that had volunteered to be a slave because of his love and respect for his master. Such a man served another man but did so out of love and devotion to the man.

We must also remember that we were not free. We were enslaved by the world, the flesh, and the devil. We were prisoners guilty of capital crimes and Messiah Jesus paid for our release and bought us with His blood. The bible tells us we will either present our bodies in worshipful devotion to sin or we will present ourselves before the Lord Jesus to serve Him (Romans 6:13).

Humanity will be a slave of something or someone. The question is not our slavery but who will be our master. Our salvation was Messiah Jesus purchasing us out of certain and eternal slavery to evil. We have been bought and paid for by His blood to be free of being slaves to such an oppressive master. Yet, our freedom is to become the slaves of Messiah Jesus.

This slavery is different. It is one where we are given friendship and adoption. We serve and acknowledge Messiah as our supreme authority, and at the same time know we have an intimate fellowship with Him. It is a slavery that makes us family.

This creates another tension for us because we normally think that if one has authority over us that this prohibits friendship with us. We normally do not feel comfortable with being emotionally intimate with our bosses. Yet, in this relationship, to not love the Lord Messiah Jesus supremely is to be a bad slave.

The movie "The Last Samurai" touched on some of these themes. The Samurai tell the Emperor "if you think that I have betrayed you, you need only command and I will gladly take my own life." The emperor was the supreme authority in the Samurai's life. To live was to serve the emperor. To die at the emperor's command was to fulfill the purpose of life. Jesus is to be our Emperor.

In the same movie, the young army captain goes from being an enemy, enslaved to guilt, to being a "volunteer servant" of the Samurai because of the respect and love he has come to have for the man. In the end, he honors his dead "lord" by being like him.

This movie is not a perfect parable for the gospel life but there are elements of it that touch upon some of the themes that we are to enter into as we strive to serve and be servants of the Lord Messiah Jesus. The combination of personal relationship, loyalty, and honor is all part of our providing loving service to Christ.

We will never be able to really experience this if our vision of Messiah Jesus is small. If Messiah Jesus is not real to us, then this will seem a call to serve an idea and not a person. Some of us feel like the Lord Jesus is just the name of our fire insurance policy. One is not deeply devoted to an insurance policy. We could never imagine making an insurance policy the supreme authority in our lives. We must come to honor and respect Messiah Jesus and see what He has done for us, if we are to ever really and fully volunteer to be under Him as our supreme authority.

How could we gain a vision of Messiah Jesus that is deeper, richer, broader, and fuller? How could we come to a place where we want to be His slave? How could our respect and love for Him grow to where we would willingly die with joy at His command?

Reading one of the gospels might help. Perhaps a deeper study of one gospel could impact us. One book; Everybody Can Know: Family Devotions from the Gospel of Luke by Francis Schaeffer and Edith Schaeffer is aimed at helping people develop a more in depth experience of the living Christ. This book helped me in the past as I sought to deepen my vision of Messiah Jesus.

Dr. James Kennedy's, founder of Evangelism Explosion International, entire life was really turned around by reading a novel about the life of Christ called The Greatest Story Every Told: A Tale of the Greatest Life Ever Lived by Fulton Ousler. That novel when read by Dr. Kennedy created a love for Messiah Jesus that never died in him. I read that same book in high school and it helped me to love Messiah Jesus more as well. It laid the foundation for my call to ministry in my senior year of high school. So this may be a book which you could help you as well.

At another critical point in my life, my devotion to Christ was renewed by the book The Cost of Discipleship by Dietrich Bonhoeffer which is largely a meditation upon the person and teachings of Messiah Jesus. This book helped me to hear the teachings of Christ in a new way. It allowed me to ask the Lord questions that were critical to my growth in faith. So perhaps reading one of these books could help you grow in our appreciation and love of Messiah Jesus.

Watching one of the classic movies on the life of Messiah Jesus might help. I know watching them every Easter on television was a family tradition for me but also a meaningful event in my faith. For some people films speak louder than words.

Some way or another, we must gain a greater vision of our Messiah Jesus if we are to be willing to actually experience Him as the supreme authority and controller of our lives. We will never be able to express love in radical service if we do not deeply know HIM.

We relate to two realities as we relate to Messiah Jesus. One reality is the biblical Messiah Jesus that we find in the Bible. Here in the inspired and true WORD, we are confronted with who Jesus the Messiah is as a person, what HE did, and what HE said. This creates a concrete and objective basis for our knowledge of the LORD. The second reality is the relationship we have with the living Messiah Jesus today. This is a subjective experience of HIS presence and leading. This is what we know in our times of prayer and meditation. This creates an intimate and subjective basis for our knowledge of the LORD. Both of these realities need to be explored.

What about you?   What events, books, films, experiences, or relationships have formed your vision of Messiah Jesus? How big is your vision?   How could it become greater?   Was it once better and now worse? What can we do to renew our vision of our Lord?   Only with a fresh vision will we be able to "serve the Lord" as an expression of our love.   Without a clear prophetic vision of Messiah Jesus, we will perish.

Prayer
Day by day, day by day, Oh dear Lord, three things I pray ; to see You more clearly, love You more dearly, follow You more nearly day by day. Amen.

My Love Goal for the Day is:

Journal for Day Eight:

Learning to Love – Day Nine – Romans 12:12

Rejoice in hope (ESV)

Let your hope make you glad (CEV)

Let your hope keep you joyful (GNB)

Be joyful in hope (ISV)

May the God of hope fill you with all joy and peace in believing, so that by the power of the Holy Spirit you may abound in hope. (Romans 15:13 ESV)

For through the Spirit, by faith, we ourselves eagerly wait for the hope of righteousness. (Galatians 5:5 ESV)

having the eyes of your hearts enlightened, that you may know what is the hope to which he has called you, what are the riches of his glorious inheritance in the saints, (Ephesians 1:18 ESV)

But since we belong to the day, let us be sober, having put on the breastplate of faith and love, and for a helmet the hope of salvation. (1 Thessalonians 5:8 ESV)

in hope of eternal life, which God, who never lies, promised before the ages began (Titus 1:2 ESV)

waiting for our blessed hope, the appearing of the glory of our great God and Savior Jesus Christ, (Titus 2:13 ESV)

If in Christ we have hope in this life only, we are of all people most to be pitied. (1 Corinthians 15:19 ESV)

Love is optimistic about the future and takes joy in God's plan. Love's focus is eternity.

We are to anticipate and expect with pleasure that Messiah Jesus will return and there will be a new heaven and a new earth in which righteousness and love will dwell. We, who are hungry and thirsty for righteousness and love, will be filled. The love of Christians for

Messiah Jesus is to lead them to want more than anything else His will to be done on earth as it is in heaven.

The gospel promises that nothing can keep the Messiah Jesus from fully and completely bringing righteousness to the earth and making His people fully loving in every way. Knowing that Christ Jesus will be exalted and God's purpose perfectly done on the earth is to fill us with joy, satisfaction, contentment, and holy happiness. Our faith in the gospel is to make us theistic optimist. We will perfectly know the intimate embrace of God in Messiah Jesus for all eternity and embrace HIM back in worshipful love. This future hope is to fill us with present joy.

Our culture believes that those who are heavenly minded are no earthly good. The heart of a secular culture is that all of life is defined and focused on "this age" and not the "age to come". Secularism views eternity as the opium of the people which keeps people from dealing with the real issues that must be solved now! The sign that we have been infected with secularism is if all of our attention is focused in the here and now and not on eternity. If we seek happiness in only temporal things, then we have become a secular person. The secular person evaluates success not by how much righteousness has been attained but by how much pleasure has been experienced in this life. For the church infected with secularism, the focus is on the health, wealth, and prosperity that God will give me today. It is not on the wonder of the second coming tomorrow, in which, I will intimately know Messiah Jesus as I have never known HIM before.

I listened to a message by Dr. John Piper which caused me to focus on Zechariah 13:9.

"And I will put this third into the fire, and refine them as one refines silver, and test them as gold is tested. They will call upon my name, and I will answer them. I will say, 'They are my people'; and they will say, 'The LORD is my God.'"

Dr. Piper mentioned in his message what Dr. John Calvin said on this verse.

*"We must at the same time learn that it is the true preparation by which the Lord brings back the elect to himself, and forms in them a sincere concern for religion, when he tries them by the cross and by various chastisements; **for prosperity is like mildew or the rust**. We cannot then look to God with clear eyes, except our eyes be cleansed. But this cleansing, as I have said, is what God has appointed as the means by which he has resolved to render his Church submissive. It is therefore necessary that we should be subject, from first to last, to the scourges of God, in order that we may from the heart call on him; for our hearts are enfeebled by prosperity, so that we cannot make the effort to pray."*

Now this is a wild concept. Our hearts are made prayer-less because they are enfeebled by physical prosperity. God helps his people by taking from them physical security and comfort so that they may trust in HIM more.

There is little doubt in my mind that the greatest Christian faith, hope, and love are found in the third world nations today. Those who have the least prosperity have the greatest hope. That is where the church is growing rapidly and joyfully. When the Apostle Paul calls upon the congregation in Rome to rejoice in hope most of them were slaves and they are living under a tyrant, Nero. How can slaves without freedom have joyful hope? Because, true hope is based in the unchanging gospel of Messiah Jesus' death for their sins, resurrection, and promised return, it is not based on good circumstances. Their joy and hope is Messiah Jesus who is the same yesterday, today, and forever.

Americans enjoy more financial prosperity and political freedom of any people on this planet. There have never been a people freer from physical needs or government oppression. Yet, we take more anti-depression medications than the rest of the world put together. We do not appear to be a very happy culture. Our secular Eden has not given us joyful hope but only anxiety over what we do not have and fear of losing what we have. We have it all; but our souls are empty of hope and all too many of us are filled with cynical anger. The gospel of secularism has not produced joy.

So what can we do? We must begin to nurture a joy based on the hope of the gospel and not just seek happiness in diversion from reality. True joy comes from focus on the reality of God's love for us in the gospel and His victory over sin. It is found by reorienting our hearts to seek first the kingdom of God and His righteousness as the prime directive of our life and entrusting God to provide for us those physical comforts we need to accomplish HIS will on earth.

Spend some time imagining the second coming today. Picture the return of Messiah Jesus in your mind. See all wars ending. All hunger ceasing. All sin stopping. Imagine perfect social justice established in every nation. See billions and billions and billions of people worshiping Messiah Jesus in wild passionate praise. See the whole earth filled with His praise. Imagine your own soul free of all sin. Read carefully the following verses from Colossians.

"If then you have been raised with Christ, seek the things that are above, where Christ is, seated at the right hand of God. Set your minds on things that are above, not on things that are on earth. For you have died, and your life is hidden with Christ in God. When Christ who is your life appears, then you also will appear with him in glory. Put to death therefore what is earthly in you: sexual immorality, impurity, passion, evil desire, and covetousness, which is idolatry. On account of these the wrath of God is coming." (Colossians 3:1-6 ESV)

Only those who are heavenly minded are any earthly good. Only a heavenly minded people can bring the rule of heaven to earth. Those who try to reach the stars may arrive at the top of the mountains. Let us find joy in the anticipation of God keeping His promises and Messiah Jesus returning paradise to earth. Let us our hope lead us to love and our love lead us to hope.

Prayer

Dear Lord, give me hope today. Help me to desire to see your will done on earth as it is in heaven. Help me believe your prophecy about the KINGDOM more than my daily dose of television news and commentaries. Save me from the cynicism and despair of our society and give to me a joyful anticipation of the future based on your unending love. Amen

My Love Goal for the Day is:

Journal Day Nine

Learning to Love – Day Ten – Romans 12:12

be patient in tribulation (ESV)

Be patient in time of trouble (CEV)

Enduring in tribulation (EMTV)

Be patient in your troubles (GNB)

Love is patient.

This passage would tell us to stay true to our faith in Christ Jesus and persevere during times when we are under pressure from difficult circumstances; such as, persecution, afflictions, disease, famine, poverty, broken relationships, loneliness, political oppression, rejection, abandonment, and abuse. We are not to flee from our love for Christ Jesus when we face hardships but to hold fast to our faith in Messiah Jesus during the hardest of times. The Apostle Paul would encourage us to be brave and not panic during times of trouble.

We live in a society that is not very patient. We do not endure a lack of pleasure or endure pain very long or very well. We live in an "instant" society and want immediate results. The idea of trusting God during hard and dark times is the opposite of what we would expect we would have to do. A call to remain faithful to God and faith even when God is not keeping bad things from happening in my life is a difficult concept. This is especially true if by the giving up of our faith we can get rid of the pressure we are under. Messiah Jesus warns that some will receive the gospel with great joy but when persecutions and hardships arise will fall away. If the roots of our faith are shallow, then that faith will not endure.

It is clear the Apostles did not have a theology that said that if a person had faith they would not have tribulation and trouble in this life. The normal Christian life is one where people struggle and suffer. Faith helps us endure the suffering, but it does not keep the suffering from coming into our lives.

We live in a time when one of the central doctrines of faith in America is that God will rapture all Christians out of the world so they will not have to suffer tribulation. It is vital to the faith of many that they will not have to endure such a time of great trouble. Now prophecy aside, what we do know is that Christians do suffer great trouble and have suffered great tribulation during all of Church history. In this year alone, an estimated 175,000 people will be killed because of their faith in Messiah Jesus. There are millions of Christians who suffer persecution under oppressive governments around the world today. They are patient in their tribulation. Regardless of our prophecy, we must be ready to endure trouble, persecution, oppression, ridicule, and poverty for the sake of Messiah Jesus. There is no promise of God that we will not suffer persecution in America before the rapture occurs.

We must learn to be patient with God and with other people. To be patient with God means that we love and trust HIM enough to believe HIS promises in the midst of painful circumstances. It also means we are committed to our relationship with HIM regardless of what happens. We are married to Lord Jesus Christ and have decided that for better or worst, in sickness and in health, and poverty and richness we will never forsake our faith. To be patient with people is to look at them with compassion and accept them as broken sinners. To have realistic expectations of others based on our knowledge of the impact of the moral fall away from God and the corruption of everything because of that rebellion against heaven. To recognize that we must wait in hope that God will help them to repent and stop their abusive behavior. Love for God and others calls us to exercise patience in both relationships.

To be patient in my troubles also means that I will not give into frustration and anger. Most of our abuse of others occurs during times when we feel under pressure. Our worst outbursts of anger come when things go wrong in our life and we feel pain. We forget that undisciplined human anger cannot make things right. The gospel calls us to bless people in our pain even as Messiah Jesus prayed for those who crucified HIM. Part of living a life of love is learning to exercise self control when we are under pressure.

Paul is really saying that true love for Messiah Jesus will endure all things. Our faith is a relationship of committed love. As we suffer various problems we need to gain God's strength in the relationship we have because of Messiah Jesus' death for our sins and resurrection from the dead. Seeing His love for us should inspire us to trust and love Him as well.

How can I increase my ability to be patient when suffering and not give in to frustration, anger, and fear? One way is to remind myself of eternity and the hope of Christ's perfect kingdom. Tribulation will not be forever. It is just a short time and then I will be free of pain and know only God's warm embrace forever. Another is to believe that there is purpose in all pain. God is at work in the trouble to bring about something good in my soul and in the world. All pain is pregnant with kingdom potential. When I know there is a purpose in my suffering, it helps me endure the pain.

Finally, my kingdom focused suffering allows me to better understand the heart of Messiah Jesus. As I take up my cross daily and suffer for God's kingdom, I become more like Messiah Jesus in HIS taking up the cross for my sins. My suffering makes me more like my Lord Jesus. So my love grows by being patient and believing in the midst of troubles.

Prayer: Lord, thank you giving me faith. Help me not doubt your love when things get tough in my life. Help me to see that the problems will not last but will give way to your eternal promises. Let me also trust that all things are working together for good. Amen

My Love Goal for the Day is:

Journal Day Ten

Learning to Love – Day Eleven – Romans 12:12

Be constant in prayer (ESV)

Continuing steadfastly in prayer (ASV)

never stop praying (CEV)

Instant in prayer (DRB)

Pray at all times (GNB)

Love prays.

The Greek work for "constant" is *proskartereo*. It is used about ten times in the New testament (Mark 3:9; Acts 1:14; 2:42,46; 6:4; 8:13; 10:7; Romans 12:12; 13:6; Colossians 4:2). Six of the ten times it is used of describing or commanding how Christians are to pray. There is emotional energy in this word. It is to feel an urgent need to be devoted to or care for someone or something. The idea is that one is in readiness to do something regularly and with passion. This is a word of discipline, devotion, loyalty, and dedication.

The Greek word for prayer is a general word used for crying out to God for help and talking to HIM in fellowship (Matthew 17:21; 21:13,22; Mark 9:29; 11:17; Luke 6:12; 19:46; 22:45; Acts 1:14; 2:42; 3:1; 6:4; 10:4,31; 12:5; 16:13,16; Romans 1:9; 12:12; 15:30; 1 Corinthians 7:5; Ephesians 1:16; 6:18; Philippians 4:6; Colossians 4:2,12; 1 Thessalonians 1:2; 1 Timothy 2:1; 5:5; Philemon 1:4,22; James 5:17; 1 Peter 3:7; 4:7; Revelation 5:8; 8:3,4). It is just talking to God. But clearly here it is talking to God sincerely and seriously.

The love for God and others that is created by the gospel in our hearts leads us to pray. Prayer demonstrates dependence on God and love for God. Prayer also demonstrates love for others. Prayer demonstrates a realistic humility about our need of God's help. We can do nothing without HIM. Prayer is to be a significant part of our lives. It is to be like spiritual breathing, where we constantly are interacting in a conversation with God. There are also to be set and regular times of prayer where we can devote

100% of our attention to God. This is to be something we regularly and faithfully do day by day. The greatest complaint that Messiah Jesus has about the worship in the temple is that it had ceased being a center of prayer for all nations. The LORD sees prayer as a vital fruit of love.

When I was born we prayed the Lord's Prayer every day in school before the start of every day. Also, every church had a prayer meeting normally on Wednesday. Now prayer has been banned by government decree from our schools and the churches have voluntary given up having prayer meetings. Prayer is hard for postmodern people to do. We are busy. We are active. Prayer is not entertaining and it is hard to see what good it does. Most people feel very frustrated with their prayer lives. The social surveyor, George Barna, tells us the following about the prayer lives of Americans.

When and how much do people pray?

An average prayer lasts just under five minutes.

52% of people who pray do so several times a day.

37% of people say they pray once a day.

33% of adults regularly participate in a prayer group or prayer-focused meeting.

21% have extended prayer time with other family members (25% among Protestants and 13% among Catholics).

It would appear that very few of us have become "constant in prayer". It would be hard to see these statistics as reflecting the devotion of the early church to prayer.

How can we become more constant in prayer? I would recommend the following ideas:

1. Dedicate a particular time and place to praying daily. Keep this appointment with God 365 days a year unless a true emergency makes it impossible.

2. Combine bible reading with prayer. Learn to pray the scriptures back to God. Also combine your prayers with singing hymns and praise songs. This will add direction and passion to our prayers. You can get hymns and praise songs off of "U Tube" and use these in your devotional time.

3. Use the Lord's Prayer as a framework to guide our prayer. Outline your prayers within the structure of the Lord's Prayer.

Deep and great prayers come from having prayer as a regular part of our lives. What could you do to become more constant in prayer? What would you recommend to a friend who asked you for suggestions on how to become more constant in prayer? What is the greatest hindrance to your prayer life? How could this hindrance be overcome? These are questions we should ponder and ask God to help us not to lose heart but to become fully devoted to being a people of prayer.

Love prays.

Prayer - Lord, give me a passion to pray to you. Help me want to spend time with you. Help me desire to praise you. Help me see that you are the source of help for everyone I care about. Give me energy to pray in a focused and loving way for others. Amen

My Love Goal for the Day is:

Day Eleven Journal

Learning to Love – Day 12 – Romans 12:13

"Communicating to the necessities of the saints" ASV

"Take care of God's needy people" CEV

"sharing in the needs of the saints" EMTV

"Contribute to the needs of the saints" ESV

"Share your belongings with your needy fellow Christians" GNB

"Supply the needs of the saints." ISV

Love gives practical help.

The Greek word for "share" or "contribute" here is *koinoneo* which means taking part in needs of another as if they were one's own. The word means to join one's self to another person and to become a partner with them. We are in partnership with other Christians and especially those who have needs. The word for "need" here is *chreia* and can be understood to "be at war to get the necessities of life"

People have five needs. We need to live. This is the needs of physical life. This command's first focus is that we need to partner with other Christians to make sure that their basic physical needs are satisfied. Some ancient manuscripts have the word "μνείαις" added to the text which means memorials; distributing to the memorials of the saints, which some interpret as referring to saints that were absent; as if he had said: "Do not forget those in other Churches who have a claim on your financial resources." This means that we need to care not only about the needs of those in our local congregation but for Christians around the world that have need of physical help. This is the primary focus of the verse.

We also need to love and be loved. If we provide for the physical needs of people but do not give to those needs with an attitude of love, then we dehumanize them. Dr. John Calvin stressed that in giving to the poor, we should never do this in such a way that would show dishonor or superiority to those in need. Some people have their physical needs met but are dying for lack of being loved. To give to each other friendship, care, compassion, and kindness are critical to meeting the needs of people. Clearly this is part of what Christians should strive to give to one another.

We also need to learn the truth. If we believe lies, then our lives suffer. There is the need of those more mature in faith to pass on the truth to those less mature in faith. There is a need to have unhealthy doctrine replaced with healthy doctrine. One of the partnerships of the church is that we are to share in the corporate wisdom of the body of Christ. We can be kept from false ideas because we are in fellowship with each other and can call each other to faithfulness to God's word.

We also need to laugh. There needs to have enjoyment and fun in the fellowship of the saints. This can be the joy of joint praise before the LORD. We share in the filling of the Holy Spirit together. We encourage each other and remind one another of God's great love. Sometimes the greatest need of our life is encouragement. Part of meeting the needs of each other is giving each other the fellowship in which our burdens are lightened.

We also need to leave a legacy. We need to try to partner with one another so that each of us will fulfill God's calling and destiny. By helping each other use our gifts and define our life purpose, we can become partners towards helping each person leave in this world what God desired. We were not called to fulfill our calling as "Lone Rangers" but only with the help and partnership of other Christians. The failure of one Christian to reach their God given legacy is a failure of the whole community. We are to be working side by side towards making every Christian a success.

What does this look like?

"The group of followers all felt the same way about everything. None of them claimed that their possessions were their own, and they shared everything they had with each other.

In a powerful way the apostles told everyone that the Lord Jesus was now alive. God greatly blessed his followers, and no one went in need of anything. Everyone who owned land or houses would sell them and bring the money" Acts 4:32-34

The early church clearly has a greater passion and vision for Christian community than we have. What can we do to better meet the needs of other believers and partner with them to see God's purpose done in their lives? How could I give to others more than I am giving now? Make a list of ways you could extend you giving to meet the needs of those in your life.

Remember, love gives.

Prayer: Lord, let me see the needs of others around me and have a heart of compassion in attempting to help others. Lord, fill me with Your love and Your willingness to serve.

My Love Goal for the Day is:

Journal Day Twelve

Learning to Love – Day Thirteen – Romans 12:13

given to hospitality (ASV)

welcome strangers into your home (CEV)

Pursuing hospitality (DRB)

seek to show hospitality (ESV)

Open your homes to strangers (GNB)

Extend hospitality to strangers (ISV)

Love throws a party.

The Greek word here would mean that a person would run after hospitality. The attitude should be that Christians are to seek to entertain people who they do not know and will not pay them back. Jesus the Messiah makes clear what his means:

"When you give a dinner or a banquet, do not invite your friends or your brothers or your relatives or rich neighbors, lest they also invite you in return and you be repaid. But when you give a feast, invite the poor, the crippled, the lame, the blind, and you will be blessed, because they cannot repay you. For you will be repaid at the resurrection of the just." (Luke 14:12-14 ESV)

When Christians celebrate, we are to have our times of eating reflect a festival that is done before the face of God. The meals are to express grace, giving, care, love, and the joy of the kingdom. Our generosity is to reflect God's generosity. Our invitation to fellowship is to reflect God's invitation to fellowship.

One way this could be expressed in a fellowship is to make sure that every visitor is invited to lunch by someone in the fellowship. My wife, Terry and I were touched by a fellowship like this in Pittsburgh. We visited a church as we had just moved to Pennsylvania. The fellowship had adopted this idea as a significant part of their philosophy of ministry. We were invited to five different people's homes for lunch. We enjoyed a wonderful afternoon with a Christian family, shared our lives, prayed for each other, and sang hymns on the piano.   It was one of those Sunday afternoons that has stuck in my mind because these people gave to us hospitality and helped us at a time when we were in need of encouragement. I thank God for that couple and that fellowship that made us feel so welcomed.   This is something that each of us can pray about making part of our lifestyle.

Another way to apply this is to give a homeless person a meal.   To give homeless people money is not wise since it normally will turn into drugs or abuse of alcohol. But to take them to McDonalds and to actually sit down and have lunch with them is a whole other story.   We could give to them fellowship and care which they normally would not have. Hospitality means more than just eating together but includes sharing our lives with each other as well. Love calls us to have an opening of hearts as well a time of mutual celebration.

The reason this is significant is that it is living out the gospel in action.   It is giving grace to people. It is what God did for us in Jesus the Messiah. We were helpless and He invited us to his banquet.

"The kingdom of heaven may be compared to a king who gave a wedding feast for his son, and sent his servants to call those who were invited to the wedding feast, but they would not come. Again he sent other servants, saying, 'Tell those who are invited, See, I have prepared my dinner, my oxen and my fat calves have been slaughtered, and everything is ready. Come to the wedding feast.' But they paid no attention and went off, one to his farm, another to his business, while the rest seized his servants, treated them shamefully, and killed them. The king was angry, and he sent his troops and destroyed those murderers and burned their city. Then he said to his servants, 'The wedding feast is ready, but those invited were not worthy. Go therefore to the main roads and invite to the wedding feast as many as you find.' And those servants went out into the roads and gathered all whom they found, both bad and good. So the wedding hall was filled with guests. (Matthew 22:2-10 ESV)

We have been saved by God's loving and graceful hospitality. This vision of grace filled living is the best way we can live the gospel. Let each of us pray about how we could act out the gospel in concrete actions.   Plan a "gospel party" of some type this next year.   Who could you invite that most needs help?   What could you do to begin showing God's love in acts of hospitality in your life?

Prayer: Lord, thank you for opening your home to me and making me a member of your family.   Your love for me is overwhelming. Help me express that love by showing generosity and fellowship with other hurting people. Amen

My Love Goal for the Day is:

Day Thirteen Journal:

Learning to Love – Day Fourteen – Romans 12:14

Bless them that persecute you (ASV)

Ask God to bless everyone who mistreats you (CEV)

Love prays for those who abuse us.

The Greek word for "bless" is *eulogeo* which in this context means that we are to ask God to do good or bless those who persecute us. We are to consecrate the persecutor to loving prayer and pronounce a blessing such as "the Lord keep you, The Lord shine his face upon you, and the Lord give you peace" or in the context of persecution "Father, forgive them for they know not what they do." We are to pray and speak this way towards people who actively pursue persecuting us for our faith, seek deliberately to mistreat us, and whose purpose in life seems to be to harass us.

Only the gospel could cause us to love our enemies like this. Such a response is the exact opposite of our normal response. Paul has moved from showing hospitality to the undeserving strangers to blessing people who do not deserve our blessing. Such a blessing would have to be given on the basis of grace alone. Even as God blessed us with forgiveness and faith while we were His enemies, now He desires we live out such radical grace in our relationships with those who make our life hard. The Apostle Paul is here simply passing on what Messiah Jesus has taught.

"But I say to you who hear, Love your enemies, do good to those who hate you, bless those who curse you, pray for those who abuse you. (Luke 6:27-28 ESV)

So how can we do this?　　How can we train ourselves to bless those who hurt us?

1. Keep your focus on being saved by grace and guard against self righteousness entering your heart.

2. Remember, that the one who is persecuting you or hurting you is made in God's image

3. Decide in times of quiet prayer to pray God's blessing upon those who have hurt you.　　This is a discipline and can become part of your planned time of prayer.　Put those who have hurt you most on your prayer list to pray for God to do good things to them.

4. Practice this on the "big persecutors" or "big enemies" which you may not have personal contact with but who normally you would not think about praying for and blessing.

Example:　Dear Father, I would ask that you will grant a heart of repentance and faith to Usama Bin Laden. Lord, have mercy on him. Send a Christian to him that can be a powerful and effective witness and save him from the false teaching of Islam. Lord, move his heart away from the bitterness and anger which has led to terrorism. Just as you loved me and saved me while I was your enemy, now save Usama Bin Laden and have grace upon him. Make him a trophy of your grace and a demonstration of your power to save anyone You will. Make him a faithful follower of Messiah Jesus who has true orthodox faith. Lord, give him faith that his sins might be forgiven. I ask this in the authority of Messiah Jesus. Amen.

5. If your "enemy" or "persecutor" is one who is a Christian, then ask the Holy Spirit to bring peace and harmony between you and them. Remember, that the one hurting you is loved by Christ and is your brother or sister in the Lord.

6. Be careful about rehearsing the wrongs done to you by this person over and over again in your mind. This normally will only lead to bitterness and anger. Be careful about the "story" you tell yourself and about "demonizing" the person in your mind. Instead, you need to pray for them and release the painful experiences to God in prayer. Only in such prayers of release can you find peace.

7. Your focus must not be "justice' but "grace". Centering on what is "fair" will lead us to anger and not to prayer.

Now, part of blessing and loving an enemy is setting a compassionate boundary up which keeps those who want to abuse us from doing more harm to us that will have to be answered for on Judgment Day. Enabling abuse is not an act of love. Yet, the boundaries can be set up without hate and anger. Indeed, boundaries need to be set up in a spirit of prayer and in the hope our enemy will become our friend.

Who is it in your life that you need to put on your "blessing prayer list"?

Prayer: Lord, help me remember that you prayed for me while I was Your enemy. When I was still Your enemy You died for me. Give me a heart to bless my persecutors and abusers. Enable me to give your grace to those who most hurt me. Amen.

My Love Goal for the Day is:

Journal Day Fourteen

Learning to Love – Day Fifteen – Romans 12:14

Do not curse those who persecute you (ASV)

Do not ask God to curse those who persecute you (GNB)

Love does not curse.

We are not to wish doom and evil to come upon our enemies. Do not pray the "cursing psalms" upon those who persecute you. This is what the Apostle Paul would have been understood as saying to the believers in his congregation who were Jewish. The inspired book of prayers has many examples of praying for those who are evil and persecute God's people to be "cursed". For Example:

109:6-20 "May his children be fatherless and his wife a widow. May his children be wandering beggars; may they be driven from their ruined homes. May a creditor seize all he has; may strangers plunder the fruits of his labor. May no one extend kindness to him or take pity on his fatherless children. May his descendants be cut off, their names blotted out from the next generation." (109:9-13)

137:7-9 "O Daughter of Babylon, doomed to destruction, happy is he who repays you for what you have done to us -- he who seizes your infants and dashes them against the rocks" (137:8-9)

139:19-22 "Do I not hate those who hate you, O LORD, and abhor those who rise up against you? I have nothing but hatred for them; I count them my enemies. (139:21-22)

Now how do we explain such prayers? Why does the Apostle now teach that such prayers as these cannot be used against those who persecute the church?

These cursing psalms were based on three good attitudes:

1. Hating evil and injustice

2. Desiring that justice be executed

3. A zeal that God's good name not be discredited by evil continuing to be allowed

Now the problem is when that fine line between justice and revenge seems to be crossed. There is one attitude in which we desire justice to prevail and another when we have so personalized the injustice that we are now expressing personal anger based on personal pain. The Apostle Paul sees this as a critical issue.

But why can we not pray the cursing psalms upon those who persecute the church. If these psalms are "wrong" then why are they part of God's prayer book?

First of all, these psalms call us to have the right attitude towards evil and injustice. They call us to have zeal for God's name, kingdom, and righteousness. These attitudes are not common and need to be encouraged. These psalms do this.

These psalms were the prayers of kings. Most of us do not have government authority. We do not bear the sword. We have not been called upon to execute justice in society. But those who are called to this ministry are literally called to battle evil many times in very concrete ways. They must be the incarnation of the "wrath of God" on earth.

So while the church, whose role is redemptive, cannot pray these prayers those who serve in the sphere of government could be called to pray such prayers especially when that government was a theocracy upon the earth designed by God himself. The kings of Israel could pray such prayers for they represented God's messianic rule upon the earth. With the end of the theocracy then such prayers would no longer fit God's will on earth or should be used by God's people upon their human foes.

The Apostle Paul also has a different perspective on those who persecute the church:

"For we do not wrestle against flesh and blood, but against the rulers, against the authorities, against the cosmic powers over this present darkness, against the spiritual forces of evil in the heavenly places." (Ephesians 6:12 ESV)

The Apostle says our battle is not against human beings but against the devil and his host of demonic powers. Physical Israel was the incarnation of God's rule on the earth and her physical battles then against pagan states became an incarnation of the demonic battle against God's kingdom on the earth. But now in the incarnation of Christ's rule is found in the person of Messiah Jesus and the spiritual fellowship of the Church who represent all nations. All nations are now chosen nations and called to follow Messiah Jesus.

Persecution comes not from human beings or even civil governments, but from the Devil himself. We can pray God's curse upon the Devil and his host for there alone is where our true enemy exists. As part of God's royal family, we can pray for the destruction of the Devil's kingdom. We should, in fact, pray that the gates of hell will fall before the witness of the Church of Messiah Jesus.

So, we are not to pray bad things upon those who persecute us, abuse us, verbally abuse us, or even physically attack us. We are to keep a heart of compassion and grace nurtured towards those who attack us. We are to pray for God to open their hearts to truth and free them from the lies of the Devil. Our righteous anger needs to be aimed at the spiritual forces behind the persecution and not the human agents of that persecution.

Now if we take this commandment seriously, it is very hard. This is not how we handle things. At the very least, we "curse" people in our gossip when they frustrate us, oppose us, or do evil against us. Sometimes, the smallest offense can create in us the deepest bitterness. This is especially true when the offense is repeated and the person is someone we see often. It is hard for us to remember that the natural human anger of a fallen sinful person cannot bring the righteousness of God to the earth. Gossip never expresses love. At best, such anger can return evil for evil. But God says; "Do not curse them and do not ask me to curse them."

How could we work towards these ends?

1. Except when speaking with a pastor, spiritual director, or counselor, never speaks evil of those who have hurt you. Speak only of their virtues and never of their vices. You can also speak to officers of the law since they are the ministers of God and are called to provide just protection. Limit speaking of the evil others do except where is necessary for justice or to find spiritual healing.

2. When speaking to a spiritual director or counselor about the evil that has been done to you seek to find a way to release your anger and not to feed your anger.

3. Do not gossip against your enemy.

4. Pray for God to convert your enemy and give them a heart of repentance.

5. Where it is possible and wise, go to your enemy and seek to make peace with them. Talk to them about the problem and seek a solution. It might be good to have a mediator or counselor help in this process.

6. Be aware of how you may have hurt your enemy and repent of any lack of love towards them.

7. Actively seek to do good to your enemy without opening yourself up to additional abuse. You have the right to set up appropriate boundaries and avoid additional attacks but you cannot attack them.

May God, help us to avoid cursing those who hurt, abuse, and persecute us. It is easy for us to wish them harm. We need to seek the heart of Messiah Jesus who when crucified on the cross prayed "Father, forgive them for they do not know what they are doing." This is what it means to live a life of gospel centered love.

Prayer: Lord, bless my enemies and keep me from cursing them in my heart. Lord, defeat the devil that is behind the pain I am feeling in this relationship. Lord, give the gift of reconciliation to m and allow me to know your peace in the midst of this conflict.

My Love Goal for the Day is:

Day Fifteen Journal

Learning to Love – Day 16 – Romans 12:15

Rejoice with them that rejoice (ASV)

When others are happy; be happy with them (CEV)

Rejoicing with rejoicing people (Literal translation)

Love knows how to laugh!

A gospel life is not a stoic life. The Stoics were people who followed a Greek philosophy in which self control was the primary virtue and emotions were seen as the primary enemy of that virtue. The Star Trek series created the "Vulcan" race that had adopted a stoic view of life and wished to be ruled by pure intellect, free of emotions. Many times people outside the church think that becoming a Christian requires them to become a "Vulcan" and lose their humanity. But one cannot live the gospel effectively this way.

The gospel is about God becoming flesh and joining humanity because HE loved us. It is a passionate story. It is a story of involvement. It is a story of feeling. The gospel is not a stoic story.

The gospel calls us to a life of empathy. Empathy is a translation of the German term *Einfühlung*, meaning to feel at one with. It implies sharing the load, or "walking a mile in someone else's shoes" which is done in order to appropriately understand a person's perspective. The gospel was about God becoming incarnate and is the ultimate act of empathy. As we live the gospel life of love we are also called to have empathy. The life of empathy is not self centered.

Within the context, this would mean that even those who persecute and curse us we should take joy in their healthy joy. If an enemy has a child born we should rejoice with them. If they gain a promotion we should share in their joy. This is one of the tests to see if we have "blessed" them. If we rejoice in their misfortune then we have been cursing them in our hearts. To bless them is to desire to see them do well and therefore we should rejoice in events of common joy shared by all human beings.

We cannot rejoice because they succeed in some evil. If their "joy" has been polluted to such an extent that they are happy in doing evil we cannot have empathy with that. God does not have empathy with our sin.

Now, it also means that in the fellowship of believers among Christians we should share in each other's "wins". When someone has a success, we should all feel successful. It should be easy to celebrate over a brother or sister having a moment of joy and happiness. This calls us to Body Life. This calls us away from being self centered emotionally. Empathy is a gift which we have to give to others. It is caring about what they care about and entering into their lives.

Practically, this normally will happen only in small groups. It is in our intimate social circles that form that we feel people have empathy with us. We have to nurture a feeling of empathy with each other. There has to be a place where people can share "the good, the bad, and the ugly" with each other. We have to hear and enter into each other's stories. We have to feel a part of their story. The Apostle Paul is calling Christians to emotional intimacy with one another. He is calling us to be friends to one another. The gospel is to create a community of friends who are bound together in empathic love.

Empathy, the recognition of the emotional states of others, requires that we imagine how others feel and what their needs might be. It requires letting go of being focused just on ourselves. It is expressed by our paying attention to people other than ourselves. It would encourage us to observe, listen, and understand others. We need to be able to truly focus on others and to read their body language and tone of voice.

To have empathy, we need self-awareness. If we understand ourselves and our emotions, we will more easily be able to understand another person's emotions. Empathy requires emotional maturity.

Now, in addition to empathy, we must also have compassion. We must care about what the other person feels and what happens to them. We must care about the other person.

This is emotional work. For many of us, this is the hardest type of work that God could call us to do. Here God commands we feel a particular way. Having empathy is godly and lacking empathy is ungodly. To fail to have empathy is a sin.

For those of us who are emotionally challenged, this alarms us. We just do not know if we are able to have empathy. God calls upon us to look upon the empathy HE had in the gospel of love in which HE became our friend at great cost. It is in this vision of gospel love that we are to find the strength to have empathy for others.

Ask the LORD to open your heart to having empathy with others and to be able to feel joy over the success of others. God's call today is to enter into the joy of other people!

Love knows how to laugh!

Prayer: Dear Lord, let me have joy over the joy of others. Allow me to rejoice when even my enemy rejoices in a healthy way. Let me desire the blessing of every person in my life and build in me empathy that I might understand them. Amen

My Love Goal for the Day is:

Day Sixteen Journal

Learning to Love – Day Seventeen – Romans 12:15

Weep with them that weep (ASV)

When others are sad, be sad (CEV)

Cry with those who are crying (ISV)

Love knows how to cry.

This verse says we should sob and wail aloud with those who are crying. We are called to openly and boldly enter into the pain of others during the losses of their lives. Here we are again called to have empathy. When others hurt we are to feel their pain. The reason for this is that the Apostle Paul wants us to be aware that we are the body of Messiah Jesus and spiritually connected to each other.

"If one member suffers, all suffer together; if one member is honored, all rejoice together. Now you are the body of Christ and individually members of it." (1 Corinthians 12:26-27 ESV)

The gospel is that Christ has died for our sins, been buried, and resurrected. The Holy Spirit has baptized us into the body of Christ and we have become members of Messiah Jesus. We have become incorporated into HIM. HIS death is now our death, HIS burial our burial, and HIS resurrection our resurrection. This baptism into Christ has united us with all other believers. We are now the body of Jesus the Messiah on the earth. This is a spiritual reality. We all share in the Life of CHRIST. Messiah Jesus has also baptized us in the Holy Spirit. We have been identified with the Son and the Spirit and they are now living in us and we are living in them.

This is an eternal relationship. This makes our union with other believers the most permanent of all our human relationships. Our relationships with other believers are the most significant human relationships in our lives. We should seek emotional intimacy with other Christians. We should desire to share their grief even as they should desire to share our grief. No Christian should ever have to cry alone.

What keeps us from knowing this type of deep emotional intimacy with each other? Many times the church is not a safe place. Many of us believe we are more likely to be judged and condemned in the church than comforted.

If we cry, we might be told that this shows a lack of faith. Other believers will dismiss our tears and tell us how they suffered far worse than that. We are more convinced that people gossip about us at church than that they pray for us. Many would tell us we caused our own pain and we are just getting what we deserve. Far from empathy, we rarely even get sympathy.

Many of us carry deep and significant "church wounds" and our relationship with the Body of Christ is defensive and guarded. When the church fails to be a safe human community then the Devil laughs with joy and Messiah Jesus cries. HIS body was to be a place of love, support, nurture, care, support, and compassion.

This is why is so important for us to develop an emotionally healthy spirituality and have emotionally healthy churches. But this is not easy to achieve. To practically create a community where real and healthy spiritual love is experienced and preserved and the normal sinful aspect of human groups is avoided is very hard to achieve. It can only be achieved when it is aimed at with great diligence, maturity, humility, and balance.

We will never have perfection but only direction. But we should be able to see a substantial difference in the life of a Christian community who has a unity in the gospel of God's unconditional love and other social groups. The gospel should bring the love of God into our hearts and change things radically. That is what we need to pray for and seek.

What could you do to have more empathy for those who are hurting today? Is there someone sick you could call? Is there someone who has suffered a loss that you could encourage? Is there someone that you could take out to breakfast or lunch? Do you need to share your own pain with someone? Intimacy means not just giving but being willing to receive.

I remember a day when I was blessed. My wife, Terry and I had another day in the hospital. Things had gone well. A new port for her dialysis was put in successfully. But it had taken longer than expected. She had become covered with blood during the operation more than expected. I took her home to clean up and then went out to get her a dinner she loves at a local restaurant. This restaurant happens to be owned by a fellow believer. As I walked in I am sure I looked a little worn out. It had been a long day and I had my worries about how things had gone. My friend happened to be there. He saw me and greeted me. He asked how Terry was doing. He expressed concern and said he would pray for us. He took my order and I waited to take it home. When he brought me the food he said "Listen, this is free; take it home, enjoy and give Terry my love." I was deeply touched. This man had seen my weariness and had responded with an act of care and love.

This was a great example of how the body of Christ can be the body of Christ. I was so encouraged and Terry was deeply touched by this act of kindness. I praise God for my brother. He became the comfort of Messiah Jesus that day to us.

How can we grow in empathy? This seems to be a critical question to which we must find the answer.

Love knows how to cry.

Prayer: Lord, give me your tears and let me open myself to godly sorrow.

My Love Goal for the Day is:

Day Seventeen Journal

Learning to Love – Day 18- Romans 12:16

Be of the same mind one towards another (ASV)

Be friendly with everyone (CEV)

Live in harmony with one another (ESV)

Have the same concern for everyone (GNB)

Love seeks healthy unity.

"Be of the same mind" comes from the Greek "*to auto phronountes*" which can be translated "thinking the same thing." The Syriac has well rendered the passage: "And what you think concerning yourselves, the same also think concerning your brethren.

Dr. Godet believes that the only possible meaning is: "aiming at the same object for one another as for yourselves"; that is to say, having each the same concern and care for the temporal and spiritual well-being of his brethren as for his own.(F. Godet, Commentary on the Epistle to the Romans (Grand Rapids, Michigan: Zondervan Publishing House, 1970), p. 436.)

This is because the word translated "mind" is "*phroneo*" which means to have and exercise the mind, sentiment, opinion, or to interest oneself in and can even mean to set the affections on. This same Greek word is used in Phil 2:2, and Phil 3:19.

"Think of, that is, regard, or seek after the same thing for each other; that is, what you regard or seek for yourself, seek also for your brethren" is what other commentators believes is the main point here. You should be thinking of others they way you think of yourself. Christian love is expressed by being united in their thoughts.

Some would focus on the need of doctrinal unity among Christians. They would urge that Christians are to think the same thing about God, humanity, and the world. There is to be a "Christian Mind" which allows Christians to have a unity within the "one faith." There is no doubt that the Apostle expects the Christian community to speak with one gospel to the unbelieving world (Galatians 1:8, 9). Part of love is to love the truth.

Others would see this as another call to empathy. This would be a proactive attitude of wanting for others in the Body of Christ what you would want for yourself. This means that we would be as concerned about the physical well being, spiritual growth, and success of others as we are for our own success. This would be what it means to love others as you love yourself.

How can we become focused on the needs of others? Only as we remember that God was focused on our needs when HE sent Jesus the Messiah to pay for our sins and give us new life in HIS resurrection. How can we love others to care about their issues as much as we care about our own? How do we lose that ultimate selfishness that makes us love ourselves above our neighbor? Only the gospel can free us from selfishness. Only when we think about how much God loved us unconditionally in Messiah Jesus can we begin to move self interest out of the center of our personal universes.

Make a list of the ten most significant people in your life. Make a list of the issues that concern each person. What are their challenges right now? Can you pray for each of these concerns as you would pray for your own concerns? Is there something you can do to help these people with reference to these challenges of their lives? How could you encourage these people as you would like to be encouraged? How can you give these people the benefit of the doubt you would like to be given? How could you become of one mind and soul with them?

Love seeks unity

Prayer: Lord, help me seek to maintain the unity of the Spirit in the bond of peace. Grant that I might care as much about the struggles of others as I care about my own concerns. Amen.

My Love Goal for the Day is:

Day Eighteen Journal

Learning to love – Day Nineteen- Romans 12:16

Set not your mind on high things (ASV)

Don't be proud and feel that you are smarter than others (CEV)

Not minding high things (DSB)

Do not be haughty (ESV)

Do not be proud, but accept humble duties (GNB)

Do not be arrogant (ISV)

Love is not proud

The Greek would most likely best be translated "Not thinking of high things". That is, not seeking them, or aspiring after them. The connection shows that the Apostle had in view those things which pertained to worldly offices and honors; wealth, and state, and grandeur. They were not to seek them for themselves. Nor were they to court the society or the honors of the people in an elevated rank in life. Christians were commonly of the poorer ranks. They were to seek their companions and joys there, and not to aspire to the society of the great and the rich.

This reflects the thought captured in Jeremiah 45:5,

"Do you seek great things for yourself? Seek them not;…".

The Lord Messiah Jesus will also warn us of having a attitude which desires the life of the rich and the famous:

"Watch out and guard yourselves from every kind of greed; because your true life is not made up of the things you own, no matter how rich you may be." (Luke 12:15 GNB)

These verses would seem to indicate that we are not to seek to become people of influence, honor, and riches. It would appear that the New Testament writers would not endorse or support the thinking found in Think and Grow Rich by Napoleon Hill.

The very things that American culture would say we should make our ultimate concerns, the Apostle Paul says are not to become the prime dream or focus of our lives. Greed and love do not mix. Love gives and greed takes.

Messiah Jesus and the Apostles would teach that we are to seek first the Kingdom of God and righteousness and not seek first fame and fortune. Our dreams are not to be the American dream. There is a real concern about the dangers of materialism found in the New Testament.

And Jesus said to his disciples, "Truly, I say to you, only with difficulty will a rich person enter the kingdom of heaven. Again I tell you, it is easier for a camel to go through the eye of a needle than for a rich person to enter the kingdom of God." (Matthew 19:23-24 ESV)

"But woe to you who are rich, for you have received your consolation." (Luke 6:24 ESV)

"And he told them a parable, saying, "The land of a rich man produced plentifully, and he thought to himself, 'What shall I do, for I have nowhere to store my crops?' And he said, 'I will do this: I will tear down my barns and build larger ones, and there I will store all my grain and my goods. And I will say to my soul, Soul, you have ample goods laid up for many years; relax, eat, drink, be merry.' But God said to him, 'Fool! This night your soul is required of you, and the things you have prepared, whose will they be?' So is the one who lays up treasure for himself and is not rich toward God." And he said to his disciples, "Therefore I tell you, do not be anxious about your life, what you will eat, nor about your body, what you will put on." (Luke 12:16-22 ESV)

The Apostle Paul makes his teaching on this subject very clear in other passages as seen below:

"Now there is great gain in godliness with contentment, for we brought nothing into the world, and we cannot take anything out of the world. But if we have food and clothing, with these we will be content. But those who desire to be rich fall into temptation, into a snare, into many senseless and harmful desires that plunge people into ruin and destruction. For the love of money is a root of all kinds of evils. It is through this craving that some have wandered away from the faith and pierced themselves with many pangs. But as for you, O man of God, flee these things. Pursue righteousness, godliness, faith, love, steadfastness, gentleness. " (1 Timothy 6:6-11 ESV)

"As for the rich in this present age, charge them not to be haughty, nor to set their hopes on the uncertainty of riches, but on God, who richly provides us with everything to enjoy. They are to do good, to be rich in good works, to be generous and ready to share, thus storing up treasure for themselves as a good foundation for the future, so that they may take hold of that which is truly life. " (1 Timothy 6:17-19 ESV)

All of this wars against the very heart of our culture. Every commercial on television screams out for us to seek to have more and get more. Wealth is the ultimate evaluation of success for most people. The American Dream has become the pursuit of material prosperity. People work more hours to get bigger cars, fancier homes, the fruits of prosperity for their families, but have less time to enjoy their prosperity. Never have any people had so much wealth and been so depressed. The pursuit of happiness has proved harder than the pursuit of wealth.

Now, every evangelical Christian will deny they have an ounce of materialism in them. We all know that being materialistic is wrong. So we are all free of this vice. Or are we? Are we sure that we have not been infected by the culture of consumerism? It is at least worth the time to pray about where our hearts really lie in regards to all of this? Are we seeking first the Kingdom of God and loving relationships more than financial security?   Are our dreams filled with living a more godly life? What we dream about normally tells us what has captured our hearts.

Love is not proud

Prayer – Lord, give me a "kingdom dream" that captures my heart and keeps me free of the "American dream" that controls my society.   Help me to be free of the love of material things. Keep me from seeking fame and fortune.   Grant to me a hunger and thirst for righteousness above everything else.

My Love Goal for the Day is:

Day Nineteen Journal

Learning to Love – Day Twenty – Romans 12: 16

Condescend to things that are lowly (ASV)

Make friends with ordinary people (CEV)

Consenting to be humble (DRB)

Associating with the humble (EMTV)

Accept humble duties (GNB)

Love is humble.

Condescend to things that are lowly is the translation of the Greek phrase "*tois tapeinois sunapagomenoi*" and can be translated; "Be carried away with (borne along with) the lowly things" or "with lowly men." The idea seems to be that we should seek to become friends not with the rich and the famous but the ordinary and unknown.

The thought is that we are not to be carried away in our minds with wanting to be part of the "rich and the famous" but rather seek the fellowship of the "faithful and the simple". There is a contrast here between an attitude of pride and one of humility. It is a warning of wanting to look like the rich and powerful.

The Greek here can be understood to mean either an impersonal state of humility or a group of humble people. Some see this as meaning that we would be content with a simple way of life as contrasted with a lifestyle of status, pride, and privilege. This would seem to be based on the teachings of Messiah Jesus.

"Blessed are the poor in spirit, for theirs is the kingdom of heaven. (Matthew 5:3 ESV)

"And he lifted up his eyes on his disciples, and said: "Blessed are you who are poor, for yours is the kingdom of God. "Blessed are you who are hungry now, for you shall be satisfied. "Blessed are you who weep now, for you shall laugh." (Luke 6:20-21 ESV)

James, the half brother of Jesus the Messiah, also seems to be concerned about us not associating with the poor as we should but rather intentionally favoring the rich.

"My brothers, show no partiality as you hold the faith in our Lord Jesus Christ, the Lord of glory. For if a man wearing a gold ring and fine clothing comes into your assembly, and a poor man in shabby clothing also comes in, and if you pay attention to the one who wears the fine clothing and say, "You sit here in a good place," while you say to the poor man, "You stand over there," or, "Sit down at my feet," have you not then made distinctions among yourselves and become judges with evil thoughts? Listen, my beloved brothers, has not God chosen those who are poor in the world to be rich in faith and heirs of the kingdom, which he has promised to those who love him? But you have dishonored the poor man. Are not the rich the ones who oppress you, and the ones who drag you into court? Are they not the ones who blaspheme the honorable name by which you were called? If you really fulfill the royal law according to the Scripture, "You shall love your neighbor as yourself," you are doing well. But if you show partiality, you are committing sin and are convicted by the law as transgressors. " (James 2:1-9 ESV)

"Come now, you rich, weep and howl for the miseries that are coming upon you. Your riches have rotted and your garments are moth-eaten. Your gold and silver have corroded, and their corrosion will be evidence against you and will eat your flesh like fire. You have laid up treasure in the last days. Behold, the wages of the laborers who mowed your fields, which you kept back by fraud, are crying out against you, and the cries of the harvesters have reached the ears of the Lord of hosts. You have lived on the earth in luxury and in self-indulgence. You have fattened your hearts in a day of slaughter. You have condemned and murdered the righteous person. He does not resist you. Be patient, therefore, brothers, until the coming of the Lord. See how the farmer waits for the precious fruit of the earth, being patient about it, until it receives the early and the late rains. You also, be patient. Establish your hearts, for the coming of the Lord is at hand. " (James 5:1-8 ESV)

When we love God and love others, we will desire to live a humble simple life and seek after a sane, stable, and spiritual lifestyle which does not evaluate success by materialistic standards. The Apostles are calling us to humble ourselves and to live a unassuming life. The Apostle James believes this is a important spiritual priority to have in one's life.

"You adulterous people! Do you not know that friendship with the world is enmity with God? Therefore whoever wishes to be a friend of the world makes himself an enemy of God. Or do you suppose it is to no purpose that the Scripture says, "He yearns jealously over the spirit that he has made to dwell in us"? But he gives more grace. Therefore it says, "God opposes the proud, but gives grace to the humble." Submit yourselves therefore to God. Resist the devil, and he will flee from you. Draw near to God, and he will draw near to you. Cleanse your hands, you sinners, and purify your hearts, you double-minded. Be wretched and mourn and weep. Let your laughter be turned to mourning and your joy to gloom. Humble yourselves before the Lord, and he will exalt you. " (James 4:4-10 ESV)

Part of humility is the ability to admit and confess our sins. It is to mourn over our transgressions. It is being able to see our lack of love and to seek to love better. It is to seek the fellowship of the spiritually struggling and weak who love without hypocrisy. It is not to seek those who seem strong, self assured, and who lack real compassionate relationships.

Another example of this can be found in the words of the Messiah Jesus who seems to contrasting these two attitudes which are found in the church of Philadelphia and Laodicea.

"And to the angel of the church in Philadelphia write: 'The words of the holy one, the true one, who has the key of David, who opens and no one will shut, who shuts and no one opens. "'I know your works. Behold, I have set before you an open door, which no one is able to shut. I know that you have but little power, and yet you have kept my word and have not denied my name. Behold, I will make those of the synagogue of Satan who say that they are Jews and

are not, but lie--behold, I will make them come and bow down before your feet and they will learn that I have loved you. Because you have kept my word about patient endurance, I will keep you from the hour of trial that is coming on the whole world, to try those who dwell on the earth. (Revelation 3:7-10 ESV)

"For you say, I am rich, I have prospered, and I need nothing, not realizing that you are wretched, pitiable, poor, blind, and naked. I counsel you to buy from me gold refined by fire, so that you may be rich, and white garments so that you may clothe yourself and the shame of your nakedness may not be seen, and salve to anoint your eyes, so that you may see. Those whom I love, I reprove and discipline, so be zealous and repent. Behold, I stand at the door and knock. If anyone hears my voice and opens the door, I will come in to him and eat with him, and he with me. "   (Revelation 3:17-20 ESV)

Again, this command which defines love is very against our popular culture. It was also against the culture of the first century. This is the reverse of what comes naturally. Only by having the mind of Christ can we begin to reflect this attitude in our daily life style.

"Have this mind among yourselves, which is yours in Christ Jesus, who, though he was in the form of God, did not count equality with God a thing to be grasped, but made himself nothing, taking the form of a servant, being born in the likeness of men. And being found in human form, he humbled himself by becoming obedient to the point of death, even death on a cross. " (Philippians 2:5-8 ESV)

To associate with the humble is to associate with Messiah Jesus. What steps could you take to build relationships with "ordinary" people? How could you serve the people in your neighborhood to show the love of Christ? How could I simplify my life and become more content with what I have?

Love is humble.

Prayer: Lord, help me seek fellowship with people not on the basis of what they have but who they are. Help me see value in those who are poor. Give to me a spirit of contentment that I might be free to love. Amen

My Love Goal for the Day is:

Day Twenty Journal

Learning to Love - Day Twenty One-Romans 12:16

Be not wise in your own conceits (ASV)

Don't be proud and feel that you are smarter than others. (CEV)

Do not become wise in your own opinion. (EMTV)

Never be wise in your own sight (ESV)

Do not think of yourselves as wise. (GNB)

Do not think that you are wiser than you really are. (ISV)

Love is aware of its own ignorance.

The Apostle Paul seems to be reflecting what was said by Isaiah.

Woe to those who are wise in their own eyes, and shrewd in their own sight!   (Isaiah 5:21 ESV)

and also the Proverb

Be not wise in your own eyes; fear the LORD, and turn away from evil.   (Proverbs 3:7 ESV)

What would this mean?   It would mean that we are not to trust in our own skill and understanding by refusing the counsel of others. Part of love is dependence.

Depending on God to instruct us is a sign that we love HIM. Depending in a healthy way on others for counsel is a sign we love them.   Having an adult to adult interdependence and not being isolated in your thinking is a mature expression of healthy love of others.

This verse would be telling us to not be headstrong, stubborn, and over confident. The ability to recognize your ignorance, lack of skill, and limited vision is a sign of emotional maturity.   Having a humble estimation of yourself allows you to love effectively. Everyone has need of help and instruction from others.   All human beings are small and inadequate.   To see this and live based on such a vision allows us to correctly love others as in need of help ourselves.

Again, this is not the way of the American culture. This is not the hero in our movies. This is not the goal we set for ourselves to be aware of our own ignorance and weakness so we can live in dependence upon Christ and HIS community of believers. Our goals normally move us to self sufficiency and independence. We have a greater trust in ourselves than we have in anyone else.

What the Apostle Paul has been focused on in this context is on our struggle with pride. Here we have an unhealthy pride in what we know and what we can do. Wisdom always included just not intellectual knowledge but practical skills of application.

The humble person knows what he does not know. The proud person pretends he knows things he does not know or believes that he knows things he does not know. Proud people are not inclined to looking within their own souls with a critical and objective eye.

Part of what causes disunity in the body of Christ is the inability to submit to each other's input. Instead of each person in the community being willing to hear others' differing opinions and trying to reach a "corporate wisdom" or "team answer", we quickly judge anyone who holds a different point of view as wrong, stupid, and inferior. Normally, there become "groups" within the church who all think alike and then stand in judgment of others in the church who are not as enlightened as obviously their group is on how things should be done. This fuels gossip, slander, and complaining. Instead of honoring each other, listening to each other, and recognizing our own need to learn, we stand in self righteous condemnation on all who disagree with us. When this grows, it leads to church splits or hostile takeovers of the church by one group over another. This is not the way of love.

Grace calls us to be humble. Grace calls us to confess we are moral failures. Grace calls us to see our need. Grace calls us to be humble. Grace calls us to see our foolishness. The gospel of grace is at war with our pride.

Self righteousness calls us to be proud. Self righteousness calls us to confess our virtues. Self righteousness calls us to see our strength. Self righteousness calls us to see our wisdom. Legalism is at war with humility.

Examine your own heart. Don't take this verse and say "Boy, does (insert name) need to apply that!" Instead, apply this to yourself and only to yourself. Each of us must deal with our own attitude of self sufficiency and trust in our own adequacy. This is not a command that calls us to judge others but instead to humble ourselves.

Love is aware of its own ignorance.

Prayer: Lord, let me know what I do not know. Help me see myself as always in need of learning. Let me be quick to listen to what others say and ready to learn from them. Give to be a teachable spirit.

My Love Goal for the Day is:

Journal for Day Twenty One

Learning to Love – Day Twenty Two – Romans 12:17

Render to no man evil for evil (ASV)

Don't mistreat someone who has mistreated you (CEV)

Repay no one evil for evil (EMTV)

If someone has done you wrong, do not repay him with a wrong. (GNB)

Love does no evil.

Render to no man is from the Greek phrase "*mēdeni apodidontes*" which can be translated. "Giving back to no man." And this is followed by the Greek pharse "*kakon anti kakou* "which means " evil for evil."

The motto of the royal arms of Scotland is in direct opposition to this Divine direction which is "*Nemo me impune lacesset*", which is translated "I render evil for evil to every man."

But wait a minute. Isn't it just to render evil for evil? Where is justice in this?

Justice is when one who is not the victim protects the victim and society by punishing one who does evil. But such action is taken by those who can be objective, fair, and balanced because they are not personally the victims. As those who have suffered evil, we are ill equipped to seek justice and well equipped to seek revenge. Justice is good. Revenge is evil. It is important that we can distinguish between the two.

Justice versus Revenge

Justice	Revenge
Objective	Subjective
Protects the innocent	Attacks
Defensive	Offensive
Impersonal	Personal
Goal is fairness	Goal is inflicting pain
Not exercised by the victims	Exercised by the victims or their friends
Selfless	Selfish

The Apostle Paul believing the teaching of the Messiah Jesus tells us that we cannot seek personal justice. We must trust in others to be our protectors such as the government or others in authority that will provide protection when we need it from those who abuse us.

This does mean that when we do evil things in reaction to other people doing evil things to us, we are not justified in this. A person once had gossiped about me and caused my reputation harm. What they had said was false. When confronted they said "Yes I was wrong in this but ...." The "but" then excused them because they felt I had hurt them and their gossip was their way of protecting themselves. They could not see and have not seen to this day that regardless of what I did, nothing could justify their gossip. Gossip is not justice; it is sin.

Another distinction here is that this is returning a moral evil for a moral evil. Someone abused me so I will abuse them. I justify my abuse because I was abused. My gossip, lying, slander, cursing, hitting, and hating are justified because it is a reaction to your gossip, lying, slander, cursing, hitting, and hating. Now both sides in an abusive relationship follow this line of thought. Normally no one feels guilty because we blame shift our responsibility to others. We are all victims just fighting to survive. Doing evil in order to not be destroyed is the main way all evil is justified. We do evil to survive; and therefore, justify the evil we do.

Evil is always evil. There is no justification for abuse. Abuse is always wrong. When we return evil for evil then evil is the winner. The fact that it is our evil "wins" does not really matter except to us. Doing evil is never an expression of love or the gospel. Doing evil does not reflect grace.

We did evil to God and God repaid us by having His SON die on the cross for our sins. While we were yet sinners, Christ died for us. We are to live the gospel of grace and love. Revenge is not part of God's will for our life or the right expression of the gospel. We must gain self control and refuse to react to evil with evil.

Love does not take revenge.

Prayer: Lord, keep me from abusing other people in my life. Keep me from justifying my wrong words, attitudes, and actions because of what they have done. Help me see how you gave me grace and let me find a healthy way to show grace to others in my life. Amen

My Love Goal for the Day is:

Journal for day twenty-two.

Learning to Love – Day Twenty-three – Romans 12:17

Take thought for things honorable in the sight of all men. (ASV)

Try to earn the respect of others (CEV)

Providing good things, not only in the sight of God but also in the sight of all men (DRB)

Providing that which is good before all men (EMTV)

Give thought to do what is honorable in the sight of all (ESV)

Try to do what everyone considers to be good (GNB)

Focus your thoughts on what is right in the sight of all people (ISV)

Provide things honest in the sight of all men (KJV)

As similar idea is found in 2 Corinthians

for we take thought for things honorable, not only in the sight of the Lord, but also in the sight of men. (2 Corinthians 8:21 ASV)

Love designs a beautiful and noble life style.

This verse tells us to plan thoughtfully and carefully to design a lifestyle and response to evil that is beautiful, noble, and morally good before a watching world.   We are to be concerned about the public testimony we give to a cynical and unbelieving society.   We must never be seen as returning evil for evil.   Our lifestyles are to be well thought out and planned to be expressions of love and respect towards all human beings and especially those who do evil to us. The gospel calls us to live a life which expresses beauty in our human relationships.

This is very hard to do. This is especially hard to do when conflict arises. We like to win in conflicts.   We feel justified in working hard to get our way when we have different views, feelings, goal, and desires than others. We will many times do anything to win in a disagreement. We normally do not plan and design how to do good but just react to circumstances without much thought.   Most of these reactions do not express love.

To fail to love we do not need to plan. We might plan to be abusive but most of the time we can just spontaneously generate evil and hurtful actions and words. Only when we are in an extremely wicked state of mine do we plan to do wrong and hurt others ahead of time.

To do what is good, noble, honorable, and beautiful in human relationships takes thought and planning. We must choose a good response instead of just having a foolish reaction. We must think before we speak. We must plan the conversations. We must control every word and action. We must pray for God's wisdom and strength to do the right thing.

To speak and act spontaneous invites abuse and evil to dominate our relationship most of the time. It is easy to do what is hurtful; it is hard to live well. We can easily be unhealthy in our relationships but it is hard to have healthy relationships.

This is the price of living in this age dominated by the spirit of rebellious and unloving Adam. We must seek the Spirit of Messiah Jesus to free us from this dark pollution of relationships and soul. Only the love of Christ will produce in us a lifestyle that is beautiful, noble, and good.

We live in a time of great moral betrayal. Bible college presidents fornicate with students, elders commit adultery against their wives, missionaries betray each other on the mission field by sleeping with the other's wives, leaders who spoke against homosexuality as a sin commit homosexuality, those attempting to shut down strip joints sleep with prostitutes, and people are conned out of their money by religious leaders for selfish purposes. The church has not seemed to have a well thought out plan to live lives of beauty, nobility, honor, and goodness before the watching and unbelieving society.

Many times as the secular society watches people in churches act in abusive and wrong ways they use this to justify their lack of faith. There is gossip, slander, and dirty politics in the church. Christians do sue each other in civil courts. The atmosphere of many churches is not one of a loving community but of a toxic waste field with many relational land mines. People do not feel safe in the fellowship and walk carefully among their fellow believers expecting at anytime something to explode. This is one reason 70% of people who claim to be "born again" do not attend church. This does not justify their not attending. But it is a partial explanation of it.

Now, it is important to remember, that the church that Paul lived in was no different. Paul himself will be slandered, subjected to gossip, and have to deal with dirty politics in the early church. People who are in the churches will be sleeping with their mother in laws and visiting prostitutes. It is clear that the real church is a broken fellowship of professing believers and will be plagued by all the dark and perverted human struggles. We must learn to love and embrace the real church and not the ideal church. But we must remember our goal is to be the ideal. Direction is important even when perfection cannot be attained.

We must plan to do the right actions and use right words in our human relationships. We must plan to act consistently with love. We must put energy into giving grace and forgiveness to each other.

Sit down and think about the relationships in your life. Think about the relationships in the body of Christ. Which of them are broken and dominated by evil? Do you have enemies? How can you plan to respond to the pain, hurt, and sin in these relationships in a sane, stable, and spiritual manner? How would you design actions that would help and not hurt these relationships and people? How could you give love to these people in a way that the watching secular society would notice? Write up a "blue print" of putting noble and right actions and words into these relationships. May God give us wisdom to know how to love.

Prayer: Lord, help me to plan to do right and not just keep reacting to people in my life. Grant to me the ability to plan a response of sane and stable love. Fill me with the Holy Spirit and give me your love for those I am in conflict with. Amen

Love Goal for this day

Journal for day twenty-three

Learning to Love – Day twenty-four - Rom 12:18

(ASV) If it be possible, as much as in you lieth, be at peace with all men.

(CEV) and do your best to live at peace with everyone.

(DRB) If it be possible, as much as is in you, have peace with all men.

(EMTV) If possible, as much as depends on you, keeping peace with all men.

(ESV) If possible, so far as it depends on you, live peaceably with all.

(GNB) Do everything possible on your part to live in peace with everybody.

Norm Wise Translation: If within your power, as far as it is dependent upon you, direct that which comes out of you to be free of aggressive and destructive attitudes and seek loving harmony with all human beings.

Love seeks peace.

Peace and love go together the same way hate and wars are friends. Love always seeks peace, forgiveness, grace, mercy, and reconciliation. The Apostle Paul is here saying we are to be peace makers. We are to be striving to find ways to live in harmony with each other and not seek destructive conflict, revenge, and bitterness.

Why is that so hard? One reason is because we make achieving goals a higher priority than loving people. There are things that we want to see achieved.   Gaining these things becomes for us the symbol of "success" and so we begin attempting to reach them.

The goals we choose may be wonderful and noble. They can be good goals. However, when people become obstacles to us reaching those goals, we then find ourselves in conflict with people. It seems like we have to go to war with them in order to gain our objectives.

Relationships are sacrificed for the good of reaching the "goal" of the organization or just our personal goals. We justify making war with others because of the need of reaching our goals.   We think that reaching this particularly important goal justifies our abusive behavior.

The first time I remember doing this was in my political days. I had built a political organization in high school. There were two people who were just not as "dedicated" as they should have been to "the cause". They were good friends of mine. Yet, because of "the cause", I would treat them in a disrespectful way to get them out of the organization. This did make the organization more effective. But the cost was much too high. I still mourn over that.

Goals can be good things. But we must reach our goals without abusing people. We must always see relationships with people as an end in themselves and never as a means of attaining an end. If we have to abuse people to reach our goals then we need to accept failure as the better option. True success is to be a peace maker. May God help me to remember this the next time I am chasing a goal.

Another reason this is hard is because it is hard for me to want others to win as much as I want to win. Instead of seeing that real success is only when everyone succeeds we then have a tendency to think that only one person can win and others must lose. Our competitive mind frame creates a win/lose universe. We, therefore, seek power and control over others and circumstances to ensure we win. This again leads to conflict and abuse. Even when we believe our "win" will be better for those we are in conflict with, this still leads us away from peace and into hurtful and unhealthy confrontation.

It is also necessary to be quick to listen and slow to speak. Many conflicts are due to a misunderstanding. We read minds and make assumptions. Recently a person told me that they knew what I believed more accurately than what I knew what I believed. They had a better understanding of my heart than I did. Now maybe they were right but because of their "insight' they did not have to listen to me. They already knew that I had an evil attitude and was just so self deceived that I could not see it. Clearly, that does not create many bridges upon which to build peace. Playing the "mind reading game" is not an effective method of "peace making". Most of us do not appreciate when others read our minds and tell us what we think or feel.

Some people think they have a spiritual gift of "discernment" or "prophecy" which allows them to judge the heart attitudes of others. It also seems to justify gossip. This type of super spiritual gossip does not build peace in the body of Christ and needs to be avoided.

There are no good biblical examples where on a regular basis God was giving people the ability to know what others were thinking or feeling. Miracles could happen but the reason they are seen as miracles is that they are rare. We need to be very cautious before we start declaring that God has told us the truth about others. Somehow, all of this "discernment" and "prophecy" is normally negative. It would appear that "God" rarely has any words of encouragement or praise for us.

There is a ministry called "Peace Makers" which provides helpful tools for individuals and ministries to increase the power we have to make peace with each other (http://www.peacemaker.net). It would be good to review their material and pray that God would help us to be more effective peace makers in our own lives. Having practical tools can help us be more successful in finding peace in our human relationships.

Now being a peace maker will not keep you from relational sins. We all blow it. At times we speak words we should not have spoken. We do things we should not have done. We fail to do things we should have done. We fail to speak words we should have spoken. All have sinned and come short of the glory of God.

The question is how do we deal with it when we sin and others sin? Do we confess our sins and seek reconciliation or deny our sin and justify our actions. Do we forgive and reconcile or isolate and gossip. The way to relational peace is confession and forgiveness. The way to relational war is self justification, isolation and gossip.

Even on the day I wrote this I failed in a conversation. I spoke words I should not have spoken. I said them in a tone I should not have said them in. I hurt a dear friend. I am so very sorry for that failure on my part. I was not an effective peace maker when I spoke those words.

I did confess and am seeking reconciliation. That is all I could do. That does not take away the pain and hurt I caused my friend. It does not justify my words. There is no justification for my words. But it is all a broken sinner can do once they sin. Everything depends on grace to heal. Peace and love is preserved by grace alone.

(ASV) Wherefore receive ye one another, even as Christ also received you, to the glory of God. (Romans 15:7)

(CEV) Honor God by accepting each other, as Christ has accepted you. (Romans 15:7)

The community of faith must find relational peace by the application of the gospel of grace. Because God has forgiven us we must strive to forgive each other and try to preserve the peace of the God found in the Church. May God have mercy upon us and help us to find the grace to give to others when they sin against us.

Prayer: Lord, make me a peace maker in the body of Christ today. Keep me from hurtful actions and words. Lord, give grace to my friends and family to be able to forgive me when I sin. Amen.

Love goal for today.

Journal for day twenty-four

Rom 12:19

(ASV) Avenge not yourselves, beloved, but give place unto the wrath of God: for it is written, Vengeance belongeth unto me; I will recompense, saith the Lord.

(CEV) Dear friends, don't try to get even. Let God take revenge. In the Scriptures the Lord says, "I am the one to take revenge and pay them back."

(DRB) Revenge not yourselves, my dearly beloved; but give place unto wrath, for it is written: Revenge is mine, I will repay, saith the Lord.

(EMTV) Beloved, do not avenge yourselves, but give place to wrath; for it is written, "Vengeance is Mine, I will repay," says the Lord.

(ESV) Beloved, never avenge yourselves, but leave it to the wrath of God, for it is written, "Vengeance is mine, I will repay, says the Lord."

(GNB) Never take revenge, my friends, but instead let God's anger do it. For the scripture says, "I will take revenge, I will pay back, says the Lord."

Norm Wise paraphrase: Beloved fellow Christian who is suffering from someone abusing you, do not seek to take justice into your own hands. Create a space for God's just anger against your abuser to be your protection and shield. As it is written in Deuteronomy 32:35 "Vengeance is mine, and recompense, At the time when their foot shall slide: For the day of their calamity is at hand, And the things that are to come upon them shall make haste. "

Love never tries to get even.

To give grace filled love to others we must not want to personally get back at those that hurt us. We must not want to harm those who have harmed us. We must surrender to God matters of justice. We must divorce ourselves from wanting revenge.

"A man that studieth revenge keeps his own wounds green, which otherwise would heal and do well"

Francis Bacon, Sr.

"Those who plot the destruction of others often perish in the attempt." Thomas Moore

Justice is the government or the church punishing someone for abusing us. Revenge is us hurting someone who hurt us. God brings justice directly by providence and through the institutions of government and church. We, however, do not have the right to exercise our own justice. The gospel is radical here. God had Christ die for His enemies.

Grace has been given to the world in order to establish the kingdom. The gospel tells us that the demands of Justice must be paid in full. But we must not take the role of government in our own hands and hurt our enemies when they hurt us.

We do not need to train ourselves to desire to take revenge. It is an immediate reaction to any abuse we suffer. We are ready to respond in kind. To return hurt for hurt. We live in a world where our emotional defense reactions can easily be based on "Mutual Assured Destruction" or M.A.D. It would appear to me that this is a policy dedicated to revenge and not justice. Some would argue that only the fear of revenge keeps people from abusing us. It is easy for us to believe that fear of us hurting others in retaliation is what keeps others from hurting us.

We do need to train ourselves to prayerfully not return hurt for hurt. It is very hard not to react with abuse when we are abused. To not claim our rights to cause pain to those who have caused us pain seems contrary to common sense. The teaching of Messiah Jesus challenges us to apply grace and love in radical ways in our human relationships.

"You have heard that it was said, 'An eye for an eye and a tooth for a tooth.' But I say to you, Do not resist the one who is evil. But if anyone slaps you on the right cheek, turn to him the other also. And if anyone would sue you and take your tunic, let him have your cloak as well. And if anyone forces you to go one mile, go with him two miles. Give to the one who begs from you, and do not refuse the one who would borrow from you. "You have heard that it was said, 'You shall love your neighbor and hate your enemy.' But I say to you, Love your enemies and pray for those who persecute you, so that you may be sons of your Father who is in heaven. For he makes his sun rise on the evil and on the good, and sends rain on the just and on the unjust. For if you love those who love you, what reward do you have? Do not even the tax collectors do the same? And if you greet only your brothers, what more are you doing than others? Do not even the Gentiles do the same? You therefore must be perfect, as your heavenly Father is perfect. " (Matthew 5:38-48 ESV)

This type of attitude only can be created by meditation on the gospel of God's grace found in Messiah Jesus. To have self control in such circumstances means we be controlled by God's Spirit and be filled with His compassion. We must learn to love sinners. We must learn to trust God. We must learn to live the gospel of grace by being a people of grace.

Prayer: Lord, help my heart be filled with your attitude of grace and mercy. Help me not seek to get even when people hurt me. Teach me to set up healthy boundaries but not become bitter. Amen.

Love goal for today.

Journal for day twenty-five

Rom 12:20

(ASV) But if thine enemy hunger, feed him; if he thirst, give him to drink: for in so doing thou shalt heap coals of fire upon his head.

(CEV) The Scriptures also say, "If your enemies are hungry, give them something to eat. And if they are thirsty, give them something to drink. This will be the same as piling burning coals on their heads."

(DRB) But if the enemy be hungry, give him to eat; if he thirst, give him to drink. For, doing this, thou shalt heap coals of fire upon his head.

(EMTV) Therefore "If your enemy should hunger, feed him; if he should thirst, give him drink; for by doing this you will heap coals of fire upon his head."

(ESV) To the contrary, "if your enemy is hungry, feed him; if he is thirsty, give him something to drink; for by so doing you will heap burning coals on his head."

(GNB) Instead, as the scripture says: "If your enemies are hungry, feed them; if they are thirsty, give them a drink; for by doing this you will make them burn with shame."

Love provides the needs of the enemy.

The Apostle here suggests Proverbs 25:21-22 as the basis for an approach to our enemies that blesses instead of curses them. There are many who believe that grace is only a New Testament concept. But this response of grace cannot be seen as a radically new approach only brought to the people of God in the New Testament. Here Paul points out that this was the wisdom of the ancient proverbs of Israel. God has always been a God of grace and His people were always called upon to seek to win by grace not revenge.

Who is my enemy? My enemy is one who intentionally and consistently seeks to do me harm. This person is dedicated to hurting me.

This is different than the person who may randomly sin against me and then immediately feels regret.   All have sinned and come short of the glory of God. Every time I sin, I hurt someone in my life.

Not everyone who sins against me is my enemy. My friends will harm me but feel remorse over the harm they have caused me. The will seek to not cause me harm in this way again. My enemies will harm me and not feel regret. They will be even encouraged that their actions caused me distress. If one particular action brought pain effectively they will repeat it. My enemy wants to hurt me and win over me. My enemy is dedicated to abusing me until I am defeated or destroyed.

There is the simple straight forward enemy. They declare they are against us. They declare their hatred for us. They clearly and openly seek to hurt us for reasons that seem justified in their eyes.

Now, you also have the self righteous enemy who sees nothing wrong in their abuse of you. If they cause you pain then it is "regrettable" but for the ultimate good. These people look upon most adults as "children"; and therefore, strive to have power and control over them by manipulating them by offering them pain and pleasure in order to get others to do what they want. These people only know abusive and co-dependent relationships.

These people cannot have adult to adult relationships with others. They want people co-dependent on them and think of everyone as inferior to themselves. They see their "abuse" like the discipline you would give to a child.

This type of enemies will confuse us because they may be "our friends" while truly being our enemy. When they are giving us "pleasure" or caring for us in a parental type of way, we will feel and cared for greatly. However, the day will come when they will have to punish us for some failure on our part or to get us to do what they know we should do. All of these acts of kindness then become emotional leverage for these people to use to get us to conform to their wills. These enemies can actually "care" for us as parents care for handicapped children but they also see all their actions from the perspective of exercising "tough love" on a rebellious child.

Such people do not normally truly confess their sins to others. If they confess their sins, it will be really an accusation. For example "I did lie but you made me do that because I knew what you would do if you knew the truth." Notice that in this "confession" they justify their sin by pointing out the flaw in your character. This is not an apology; it is further abuse and attack disguised as an apology. These people are "chess players" and see everyone else as pawns on their board.

Now, the self righteous enemy can also be one who either you have hurt or who perceives you as doing something hurtful. They have decided to take revenge for that injury. They have nursed that wound until it has become bitterness in their soul. They live to hurt you and dream of the day they will take you down. They see this as the victory of justice. These enemies can also pretend to be friends if we seem to have more power than they do. They can decide a guerrilla war from within has more chance of success than a frontal attack. They will gain access into our lives in order to cause us pain or were already in our lives when they began to seek revenge.

Our friends, family, and spouses can become our enemy. This creates a dual relationship that is very mixed. On the one hand are those elements that bond us together. Good memories, mutual commitments, common experiences, promises, and the bond of blood. On the other, is the evil intention, the need to have power and control, the lack of trust or the thirst for revenge that then poisons the relationship.

These types of conflicts hurt us more than any one else. In the same way, as we have greater anger towards a traitor to our country than a enemy combatant so we feel greater pain when betrayed by a friend. The one is an enemy but we have no relationship or bond with them. But the other is a person that we expected loyalty and respect from only to be betrayed. When our inner circle becomes our enemy this causes the greatest pain we can have in our lives. Messiah Jesus knew about that type of pain.

"He was in the world, and the world was made through him, yet the world did not know him. He came to his own, and his own people did not receive him." (John 1:10-11 ESV)

Now some enemies are goal directed enemies. They have nothing against us. However, we are standing in the way of their reaching their goal. So they must get us out of the way. This normally means they will hurt us until we move. But there is nothing personal about it. It is just business. Once we move and allow them to reach their goal, then they will not hurt us anymore. But if we refuse to move they will bury us. Their goal is what they value not us.

Normally our enemy will have written a "story" about us. We are the villains of that story. In that story we are demonized and depersonalized. This internal "propaganda' fuels our enemies hatred or anger towards us. In this story only our vices will be mentioned and the emotions fueled by this story keep our enemy our enemy.

So there are many types of enemies we face. When we are hurt by an enemy, our immediate response is to hurt them back. If they curse us then we will curse them. If they gossip about us then we will slander them. If they verbally or emotionally hurt us then we will respond in kind. This is what we do without thinking about the gospel.

But when we remember the gospel then everything is different. We will speak of their virtues and refuse to demonize them. We will not speak evil of them. We will not gossip about them. The gospel of God's unconditional love calls us instead to understand and meet their most basic needs. To whatever extent we are able to help them we are to give them aid. We are to bless them and not curse them.

We are told this will put "burning coals on their head". What does this mean?

Kiel and Delitzsch in their commentary say:

"The burning of coals laid on the head must be a painful but wholesome consequence; it is a figure of self-accusing repentance (Augustine, Zöckler), for the producing of which the showing of good to an enemy is a noble motive. That God rewards such magnanimity may not be the special motive; but this view might contribute to it, for otherwise such promises of God as Isaiah 58:8-12 were without moral right.

The proverb also requires one to show himself gentle and liberal toward a needy enemy, and present a twofold reason for this: first, that thereby his injustice is brought home to his conscience; and, secondly, that thus God is well-pleased in such practical love toward an enemy, and will reward it; - by such conduct, apart from the performance of a law grounded in our moral nature, one advances the happiness of his neighbor and his own."

Other commentators see this phrase is tied to Lev 16:12 in which the burning coals were tied to prayer, forgiveness, and reconciliation. The key here is that such an action lives out the gospel of grace and love in a concrete way in the midst of the hard issues raised when we face an enemy. It also suggests that the best way to handle an enemy is to love them. This is not a promise that they will repent but it is a wise suggestion about how to encourage them to repent.

While some have suggested kindness as the best revenge, this goes against the spirit of the context. It seems more likely that the burning coals reflect the shame that comes when our enemy sees we are not doing evil to them. Any sense of justice and fairness are destroyed when we do acts of kindness to our enemy. We are not doing things that help our enemy justify their actions. This helps them to take a step back and get an objective perspective on what they are doing. This reality check can be used by God to help to repent.

Now, we must do this without giving our enemy undue potential to do us harm again. This is especially true when the person we are in conflict with may represent a potential physical harm to our well being. We do not love our enemy by failing to have proper boundaries up which keeps them from doing evil for which they will be held accountable on judgment day. What is a social and emotional boundary in a relationship?

A boundary is not about telling another person what to do. It is not taking an action to hurt the other person. It is about telling another person what YOU will do in the face of the other's continued unkind or undesirable behavior.

While it is hard for most people to accept, we cannot control another person's behavior. What we can control is our own response in the face of others' behavior. Part of that response has to be that we will not seek revenge. Part of that response is that we will seek to bless our enemy. Part of that response will be to set healthy boundaries. All of these actions are responses that we can choose and are 100% under our control.

For example, if someone emotionally abuses us by yelling at us then we need to simply say with love; "When you yell at me, I am going to end the conversation and walk away, because it does not do either of us any good." That is a boundary. It is not aggressive, seeking revenge, or seeking to control the other person. It is simply saying that when it is under your control you will not submit to being abused by another person. This keeps us from becoming bitter and moves towards relationship becoming better.

So make a list of your enemies. What is in your power that you can do to bless them today? You can pray for them. You can pray for reconciliation with them. You can confess your sins to them as an example of humility. You can seek to do them good and not harm today. You can refuse to gossip about them and seek to speak of their virtues. You must depend on God to reward and protect you. As Jesus the Messiah taught "love your enemies".

Prayer: Lord, give me the courage to love my enemy today. Help me be like You in giving unconditional love and compassion to those who abuse me. Help me know how to set healthy boundaries without seeking revenge. Show me how to show grace to those who hurt me. Amen

Love goal for today.

Journal for day twenty-six

Learning to love – Day Twenty Seven – Romans 12:21
Rom 12:21

(ASV) Be not overcome of evil, but overcome evil with good.

(CEV) Don't let evil defeat you, but defeat evil with good.

(DRB) Be not overcome by evil: but overcome evil by good.

(EMTV) Do not be overcome by evil, but overcome evil with good.

(ESV) Do not be overcome by evil, but overcome evil with good.

(GNB) Do not let evil defeat you; instead, conquer evil with good.

Rom 12:21
   Be not overcome of evil (mē nikō hupo tou kakou).   "Stop being conquered by the evil (thing or man),"
   But overcome evil with good (alla nika en tōi agathōi to kakon). "But keep on conquering the evil in the good." Drown the evil in the good.

Love wins.

Barnes Notes makes the following comment on this passage:

"This is the noble and grand sentiment of the Christian religion. Nothing like this is to be found in the pagan classics; and nothing like it ever existed among pagan nations. Christianity alone has brought forth this lovely and mighty principle; and one design of it is to advance the welfare of man by promoting peace, harmony, and love. The idea of "overcoming evil with good" never occurred to people until the gospel was preached. It never has been acted on except under the influences of the gospel. On this principle God shows kindness; on this principle the Savior came, and bled, and died; and on this principle all Christians should act in treating their enemies, and in bringing a world to the knowledge of the Lord Jesus. If Christians will show benevolence, if they will send forth proofs of love to the ends of the earth, the evil of the world will be overcome. Nor can the nations be converted until Christians act on this great and most important principle of their religion, "on the largest scale possible," to "overcome evil with good."

The unbelieving secular culture, the unbelief of our own heart, and the morally fallen angel called the devil who is the adversary of our souls all encourage us to not to believe that evil can be overcome with good. They will tell us that we must fight fire with fire.   We will be counseled that in the "real world" we must be as violent as our adversary in order to defeat him and keep the evil he is doing from continuing. The cost of beating evil is to do evil is the advice of a cynical culture. That is the wisdom of unbelief. That is how we normally think without the gospel of grace at the center of our hearts. Such understanding is like breathing. It comes automatically and apparently out of necessity.

Yet, the gospel says 'No' to this. We are God's enemies. He chooses to love us. We are sinners, HE sends Messiah Jesus to die for our sins. We are rebels against the heavenly kingdom and HE offers us amnesty for our crimes. God is a peace maker. God loves his enemies. God has overcome evil by doing wild acts of sacrificial kindness and compassion for HIS enemies. Those of us who have been saved by this untamed goodness by God are called to imitate this passionate grace filled compassion in our own lives. He calls us to win over evil by returning good when we suffer abuse. He challenges us to become better not bitter towards those who hurt us.

How does this defeat evil? It may cause our enemy to have a reality check and without any new provocations on our part the fire of their anger can begin to die out. Without fuel and oxygen, fires die. When we drown the evil of our enemy in words of blessing and acts of kindness, the atmosphere that normally feeds conflict has been killed. Only if our enemy has a nuclear reactor of hate within his heart for us will they be able to maintain their hatred for us. Because grace is such an unexpected response, it may overcome the evil in the heart of our enemy. In fact it is the only thing that can.

How does this work in real life? Dr. Jay Adams the Christian Counselor tells this story.

"A woman I was counseling whose husband was going away on weekends when he should have been with her decided that since he went away these weekends in camping that she would do something good for him instead of being furious and whining and complaining as she had been. So she started doing good. She'd pack weekend lunches. She'd put little surprises in his back pack. She would do all kinds of good things to make his weekend more pleasant. And it just changed everything in that home. "

Now the woman had communicated her feelings and her desires. She had communicated in love her feelings of being abandoned and rejected when her husband left her. But without denying the reality of her hurt the woman returned good to her husband. She also stopped gossiping about her husband to her friends. She stopped slandering her husband and encouraging people to think evil of him. She just started to show love towards her husband. She continued to suggest some win/win solutions to how weekends could be handled. Yet, she kept herself from becoming bitter towards her husband and this helped her husband to hear her.

There are many balances to this. Doing acts of kindness is not enabling evil. We still call evil, evil. We do not deny our pain. We do not deny that abuse is occurring. We do not fail to set up healthy boundaries which will keep abuse from occurring, but these boundaries are passive and defensive, not aggressive in nature. Part of loving another person is not encouraging them to be abusive by failing to have structures in place in our relationship that limit the potential for abuse. We do not stop seeking win/win solutions. So there is a balance that needs to be maintained here.

But the radical part of this strategy is that we proactively seek to do positive and compassionate acts of kindness to those who abuse us. We pray for them. We seek ways to help them. We strive to make sure their needs are met. We love them in concrete and real ways. We refuse to become bitter. We refuse to return evil for evil. We refuse to abuse those who abuse us.

One can see this in the different approaches to Germany at the end of World War I and World War II. At the end of World War I there was a desire to return evil for evil. Germany had led the world into a war that crippled a generation. The allies decided they had to pay for their evil and most people believe that decision created the atmosphere that enabled the German leader Adolf Hitler to gain power. Returning evil for evil produced more evil.

After World War II, the allies decided to rebuild Germany under the Marshall plan. This led to a more stable environment and better economy. We returned good for evil and at least to some extent evil was overcome. This is a good example of what is called "soft power" in political theory, which we sometimes hear about in the news today. This is a historical example of how returning good for evil stopped the cycle of evil and brought about a better state of affairs.

But what if I return good for evil and the other person continues to abuse me? How has good overcome evil then? Even when our drowning the other person in good does not change them; it has changed us. The greatest evil another person can do to us is encourage us to become evil ourselves. That is damage to our souls.

When we return good for evil we demonstrate the limitation of the power of our enemy. Our enemy cannot make us evil. Our enemy cannot corrupt our souls. We are free of our enemy's power as long as we choose to do good. Evil is defeated because it does not spread. Like a quarantined computer virus it is now contained and controlled. Living by the love and grace of the gospel makes us immune to the plague of sin. Evil is defeated by gospel love.

Take a step back from your life. Get an objective view of your relationships. Who are your enemies? How could you drown them in good today? This is a war. Our greatest weapon is love.

Love wins.

Prayer: Lord let me trust in the power of love to win in the battle against evil. Let me not trust in doing evil to save me from evil. This is insanity. Help me be sane enough to see that only grace, compassion, and forgiveness can actually defeat abuse and hatred. Teach me to imitate the gospel in my relationships and give kindness to those who hurt me. Help me to set up healthy boundaries that will limit destructive patterns in the relationship. Grant to me to be able to love with true wisdom. Amen.

Love goal for today.

Journal for day twenty-seven

Conclusion

If I speak in the tongues of men and of angels, but have not love, I am a noisy gong or a clanging cymbal. And if I have prophetic powers, and understand all mysteries and all knowledge, and if I have all faith, so as to remove mountains, but have not love, I am nothing. If I give away all I have, and if I deliver up my body to be burned, but have not love, I gain nothing. Love is patient and kind; love does not envy or boast; it is not arrogant or rude. It does not insist on its own way; it is not irritable or resentful; it does not rejoice at wrongdoing, but rejoices with the truth. Love bears all things, believes all things, hopes all things, endures all things. Love never ends. As for prophecies, they will pass away; as for tongues, they will cease; as for knowledge, it will pass away. For we know in part and we prophesy in part, but when the perfect comes, the partial will pass away. When I was a child, I spoke like a child, I thought like a child, I reasoned like a child. When I became a man, I gave up childish ways. For now we see in a mirror dimly, but then face to face. Now I know in part; then I shall know fully, even as I have been fully known. So now faith, hope, and love abide, these three; but the greatest of these is love. (1 Corinthians 13:1-13 ESV)

Final Journal

Set a day aside to reflect on what you have learned and processed in this book. Go to a safe and nurturing place where you can think and pray. Read each of your journal entries slowly. Read anything that you underlined in the book. Pray about what you have written and pray about what you have underlined. Take time to meditate about what it would mean to live a life of grace filled love.

Now set some bigger life style goals. How will you change your normal way of doing things?

What habits in your relationship with God have to be changed?

What habits in your relationships with people have to be changed?

 What have you learned about love that you can apply in a new way into your life?

I pray that this process will help you to learn to love more and more effectively for the rest of your life.   Amen

Notes

Journal for a day of reflection

43088910R00077